True Leadership

*How you can provide it and
become secure, happy and rich!*

Jan Ruhe
and
Art Burleigh

PROTEUS
PRESS
Aspen, Colorado

Published by PROTEUS PRESS
300 Puppy Smith, Suite 205-290
Aspen, Colorado 81611

Publisher's Cataloging-in-Publication Data
Ruhe, Jan.
    True leadership: how you can provide it and become secure,
    happy and rich! / Jan Ruhe, Art Burleigh. – Aspen, CO : Proteus
    Press, 2000.
        p.   cm.
    ISBN 0-9702677-0-7

    1. Leadership.   I. Burleigh, Art.   II. Title.
HD57 .7 R84   2000   00-107926
658. 4/092   dc—21   CIP

03 02 01 00 ❖ 5 4 3 2 1

Printed in the United States of America

From the bottom of our hearts, everything we have done is to improve the lifestyle for others, including our families.

To the wind beneath our wings—you have filled our lives with abundant joy and happiness:

Seth and Marlyn Burleigh

Sarah, Clayton and Ashley White and Bill Ruhe

Contents

Preface
It's Later Than You Think

FRANK KEEFER

N EWS OF JOHN KALENCH'S DEATH HIT ME LIKE A bullet between the eyes! No, more like a lance through the heart. He was not only a good friend, but also an industry giant.

I have no doubt that in the short time that he was with us he accomplished his life's goal of creating a million friends.

At a minimum, he changed the lives of tens of thousands through his seminars and books.

I know, I was one of them.

I celebrated his knowledge and experience by giving away his books by the case to both distributors and prospects as well.

Although we talked occasionally on the phone, the last time that I saw John was at a Master's Seminar we did in the Northwest a while back.

John and I shared a common bond. The medical community had written us both off.

At the time, I was barely holding my own, but miraculously John was in remission from a cancer that is fatal in nearly 100% of the cases. I was ecstatic for him.

John's passing, along with the deaths of two other friends this week, all younger than me, brings to the forefront my own mortality and an adage that my uncle has drilled into my head for decades: "It's later than you think!"

I don't know how much time I have left.

Neither do you.

The difference may be that as a result of my experiences as a combat Marine and later as a U.S. Army Special Forces operative coupled with seven years spent in emergency rooms and operating rooms . . . I may understand it better than you do.

Early on I developed a sense of urgency that I brought into my network marketing business.

If you don't have a sense of urgency, you need to develop one . . . and, you need to do it quickly!

It's later than you think!

If you are complacent, you're defenseless.

You are positioning yourself to be controlled by unforeseen circumstances in the future. Why not become proactive now and prepared for eventualities outside of your control later?

Several years back I had three folks in my organization, two personally sponsored, who were battling catastrophic illnesses. The cases were heartbreaking.

None of these folks developed a sense of urgency about their business when they had the opportunity.

When they became terminally ill, they were panic stricken over the financial future of their families.

Early on, before they were consumed by disease, I had encouraged them to get serious about their business.

Their responses were universal.

"I don't have the time."

All I could do was shake my head sadly.

I knew what they didn't know and didn't want to hear. "It's later than you think!"

Within weeks of each other they awoke one day to find that they had terminal cancer. Suddenly, faced with their own mortality, their family's financial future took on a whole new meaning.

But, it was too late. They had never treated the opportunity seriously. With tears in their eyes, each came to me begging for an answer as to how they could build the business overnight.

Nothing is built overnight.

This business is built showing the plan one presentation at a time, one distributor at a time.

There was nothing that I could tell them.

Sacrificing a little time and money now for higher quality time and a more solid financial picture in the future was a concept they never understood.

I'd tell them that "it's later than you think", but they wouldn't believe me.

Three years ago, without warning, I nearly expired due to congestive heart failure and surrounding complications.

I was admitted to the hospital in critical condition with a blood pressure of 45/20. I was minutes from death.

It took several days to get me stabilized but the damage was done. My heart muscle was irreparably trashed.

I was told that it would never again operate at greater than 15%. My life expectancy was measured in weeks, a few months at best. I was told I'd never work again.

My activity for evermore was not to exceed 10 minutes every other hour.

I was finished!

The greatest solace to me during those dark days was that I was debt-free and had built a solid network marketing business that would not only pay me residually while I was alive, but would take care of my family after my death.

Where would I have been if a few years earlier I hadn't exercised the sense of urgency necessary to build my business?

Most likely, I would have been relegated to a few bucks a month of social security disability, probably would have had to sell my home and move into a low rent apartment in some seedy neighborhood and wait around to die.

You know how stuff happens to the other guy?

Guess what? It happened to me!

And, at some point in your life, it will happen to you.

You will be the other guy. You just don't know when.

In my case it was heart trouble.

In John's, it was cancer.

It shouldn't have happened.

Both of us were physically fit and nutritionally conscious.

Oh well! It could just as easily have been an auto wreck, a fatal fire, random street violence or some other equally devastating situation. You're not immune.

Wake up to the fact that it's later than you think.

You have no time to waste.

Get your butt in gear! Make it happen!

A successful network-marketing career is the cheapest insurance policy you'll ever get.

The premium is a little effort put forth to help others.

That effort that you put forth today is your down-payment for your family's security tomorrow.

It's later than you think!

We Remember

Network Marketing Industry *True Leaders:*

Mark Hughes ~ *Herbalife*

Ken Pontious ~ *Enrich International*

John Kalench ~ *Nikken, Inc. &*
Millionaires in Motion

Foreword

Kelton Drew Earl

WHAT WOULD IT BE WORTH TO YOU IN DOLLARS AND cents, to sit down with a millionaire networker who has the time freedom, money and the lifestyle you desire? One hundred dollars? Two hundred dollars? I once had such an opportunity. I would have willingly paid all I had at the time to be able to listen firsthand to the leaders who had made it big in a home-based business. But as fate would have it, I only had to meet at a fine hotel and pay for my own dinner in an exquisite restaurant. This was a small price to pay for such a rare opportunity.

During the evening, he poured out buckets of wisdom and experience on me. I absorbed all that I could, fighting the temptation to take out a pen and write notes on the white tablecloth.

What I learned that evening surprised me. I already knew a great deal about how to build a successful business, he just confirmed for me that I could succeed. What I was not so aware of was what *not* to do, and what pitfalls to avoid. Home-based businesses are built on proven principles and techniques that in most cases are honed to an art. Successful people have blazed a trail before us, have left us the plan to follow, and for the most part our job is to follow these strategies.

But what about those things that blindside us, delay our success and dampen our dreams? What about those events, distractions or people who would rather have us fail than succeed? Are we prepared for them? Dr. Jim Seitz, who holds a world record in first month earnings in multi-level marketing, spoke at a meeting in Phoenix, Arizona. He said, "I have found in our business, that it is not the ups and downs that get to you, it is usually the jerks along the way!"

As I listened to my millionaire teachers that evening, I realized that we must be alert to the dream stealers, and non-leaders as we build our dreams. I later wrote a book, *The Psychology of Network Marketing*, and coined a title for the fake diamonds that surround us. I labeled them "Zirconias."

I wrote that in the wealth building industry, we enjoy one of the noblest professions available to entrepreneurs today. We share with people a future free of debt and free of the shackles of being broke. I expounded on the type of person who will steer you away from your success, and why they do this. In getting feedback from stars in the industry, I soon learned that all the upper level leaders of the MLM/Network Marketing world share the same concerns about how important it is to avoid making mistakes.

Jan Ruhe, the celebrated author of *MLM Nuts $ Bolts* and *Fire Up!*, spoke at a conference in Las Vegas, where I also was a speaker. Our times were conflicting, so we did not get a chance to meet, but I left her a copy of my book and requested her review. Not unlike my first opportunity to interview a successful distributor, Jan contacted me and agreed to give me her feedback, if I would visit her and her husband Bill at their lovely home in the Colorado Rockies. We formed a friend-ship, and found that we share much the same ideals and desire to set people free through home-based business oppor-tunities.

Jan is now carrying the torch even further with *True Leadership*. What Jan and Art have done here is provide you with the in-depth insight that you will need to move forward with your success plan, things to watch out for, and ways to identify those who will go with you into the winners' circle. Here is your dinner with the pros! Here is your insider information to help you make the big time in your quest. And the cost? Well, how much would you pay for a one-on-one to hear what is written here? It would be the same information, but you don't have to leave a tip!

The contributors to this work have offered you all the nuggets of wisdom you will need to be at the top. I suggest, however, that as you read these nuggets, you savor the thoughts and insights, and digest the material, and you should do it in a fine restaurant in a nice hotel.

Kelton Drew Earl is a renowned expert on training Network Marketers. Since 1985, Drew has grown several successful organizations from the ground up to become a perennial record-setting distributor. He has served in executive-level sales, marketing and recruiting positions with several Network Marketing companies. He and his wife, Gabie, and their four children live in Nevada.

deark@earthlink.net

Acknowledgments

A huge and special heartfelt thank you to:

♦ **Kelton Drew Earl** for being the inspiration for this book.

♦ **John Milton Fogg** for his championing of both of us.

♦ **Jim Rohn** and **Tom Hopkins** for their contributions, as they have been Jan's mentors for over almost two decades.

♦ **Martha and Arthur C. Burleigh, Jr.** for guiding and inspiring Art for half a century.

♦ **Jay Sargeant** and **Randy Gage** for their contributions, as they have been Art's mentors and inspiration—along with Art's dear friend, **Jan Ruhe**.

♦ All the *True Leaders* of this planet Earth.

♦ All of the contributors in this book, for your willingness to contribute to *True Leadership*. Without all of you, this book could not have come together.

And it's with a gratitude attitude, to our *True Leaders* in our organizations without whom we would not have risen to the top of Network Marketing. You have lifted us on your shoulders to be *True Leaders*. However, we know the truth—it's because of you and your *True Leadership* that we have learned enough lessons to share this book.

We had a lot of fun writing this book together, thinking of you and how excited we are that you will be a *True Leader* in this new Millennium.

Introduction

The First Word on True Leadership

JOHN MILTON FOGG

WHEN JAN AND ART ASKED ME TO WRITE THE Introduction to *True Leadership*, I asked them in return to tell me the key points they wanted me to cover. They sent a list! One point jumped out at me. It read: "Endorse the idea of *becoming* a *True Leader*."

Okay. I endorse the idea—and I'll explain a little about that with a passage I wrote from *Conversations with The Greatest Networker in the World*.

"What I train about is *who to be* to be successful in this business," he continued. "That's what's really important to me and I say to you, too. That's what everybody *really* needs to know—and so very few people *really* do.

"This business is relationship *led*. . ."

He looked over at me to see if I understood and must have noticed something lacking in my expression, for he continued, "I see. Okay. You've read phrases in business books like, 'profit *driven*' or 'product *driven*'—yes?"

I replied that I had and quoted a line Benjamin Franklin once said: "Drive thy business, or it will drive thee."

"Great!" he exclaimed. "Ben Franklin said that. Far out. Well, what if ol' Ben had said instead, '*Lead* thy business, or thy business will *lead* thee?'"

When I didn't answer, he said, "Let me tell you a story that beautifully explains the difference between being *driven* and being *led*. Have you ever heard of a man named Joe Batten?" he asked me.

I told him I hadn't.

"Mr. Batten is one of the grand old men of public speaking. He's a member of the National Speaker's Association Hall of Fame and he wrote the business best-seller *Tough-minded Leadership*.

"Some years ago, Joe was meeting with a group of 35 corporate CEOs for a day-long seminar. Early in the presentation, he asked, 'How many of you are leaders in your company?' Of course, every hand in the room went up.

"Joe smiled and said, 'I'll ask you the same question *after* I share this true story with you.'

" 'In the Middle East,' Joe told them, 'there are two countries separated by a common border which each have large sheep and mutton industries. The cultures of the two countries are radically different, and they are hostile to each other. In fact, they have fought wars with each other. And they are fighting as we speak.'

" 'In one country, the shepherds walk behind their flocks.

" 'In the other country, the shepherds walk in front of their flocks.

" 'Now remember,' Joe told them, 'this is a true story.'

"Joe continued: 'In the country where the shepherds walk *behind* their flocks, the quality of the mutton and the wool is poor, and it is not a profitable industry. In the country where the shepherds walk *in front* of their flocks, the quality of the mutton and wool is excellent, and the profitability is high.'

"Then Joe asked the group, 'Why?' Nobody answered, so Joe told them.

" 'In the flocks where the shepherd walks *behind* and drives, pushes, corrects, and is always in charge, the young sheep grow up afraid to stray from the flock for fear of being rapped upside the head by the shepherd's staff or having the dogs sent out to round them up. They have no opportunity to explore for better grass and water, or to play with other young lambs. They simply become obedient, passive and apathetic. By the time they are grown, they have lost all initiative. They are not really healthy. They are *driven*.

" 'In the country where the shepherds walk *in front* of their flocks,' Joe continued on, 'the young lambs have plenty of opportunity to stray, play, experiment, and then catch up to the flock. Instead of feeling controlled, compressed, repressed, depressed, and suppressed, they feel free, empowered, enhanced, and stretched. They eat more, sleep better and grow up large and healthy. They are *led*.'

"Now, when Joe finished his story," The Greatest Networker said, "assuring the assembled executives again of its authenticity, he asked them once more, 'How many of you truly *lead* in your company?' "

The Greatest Networker turned and looked at me, asking, "Would it surprise you to learn not a hand was raised?"

The only way for anyone to achieve *True Leadership* is to be a *True Leader*. I'm well aware that what I am about to do is very "bad form" for the introduction to a book, but the truth is you cannot become a *True Leader* by reading—this book or any other. The only thing to do to be a *True Leader,* is to walk in front of your flock, being *True Leadership*.

Of course, you will learn a lot from this book. That's because the men and women whose hearts and minds fill the following pages are *True Leaders*—that's who they be.

Start with Jan and Art. They're *True Leaders*—of the first and finest order. And so are Richard Brooke, John David Mann, Michael Clouse, Rita Davenport, Connie Dugan, Drew Earl, Pam Evans, Teresa Epps, Hilton Johnson, Frank Keefer, Robert Lovell, Ruby Miller-Lyman, Joe Rubino, Tim Sales, Tom "Big Al" Schreiter, Rene Yarnell, and on and on and on. This book runneth over with *True Leaders* being *True Leaders* on pages in print. They will inform you, and involve you and inspire you all over, under, around and through *True Leadership*.

Don't look for the "How to."

Look for the "*Who to*."

And when you "get it," even just a taste of it, put the book down, stand up, take your staff in hand and stride out in front-of your flock, your organization, your family, your company, your community, your world-and be the *True Leader* every person who has contributed to this very special book knows you are.

John Milton Fogg is an author, editor, speaker and an expert on Network Marketing. His books and tapes have sold over three million copies worldwide. He is the author of the best-selling industry classic, *The Greatest Networker in the World*™, and he produced the tape albums *Conversations with the Greatest Networkers in the World*, *The Women's Tapes* and *WMLM*. John has written or edited over 24 other books and tapes on Network Marketing. He is the founder of both *Network Marketing Lifestyles*™ magazine and *Upline*® *Journal* and has served as the Editor In Chief for both publications. He is a long-time friend of Jan's and edited her first two best-selling books. Art has also known John for several years and participated in John's first Greatest Networker™ Mentor Program. John Fogg lives in Virginia.

Jmf@GreatestNetworker.com
www.GreatestNetworker.com

❧ Nelson Mandela ❧

1994 Inaugural Speech Excerpt

Our deepest fear is not that we are inadequate.
Our deepest fear is that we are
powerful beyond measure.

It is our light, not our darkness that most frightens us.
We ask ourselves, who am I to be brilliant,
gorgeous, talented and fabulous?

Actually, who are you not to be?

You are a child of God.

Your playing small does not serve the world.
There's nothing enlightened about shrinking
so that other people won't feel insecure around you.

We are born to make manifest the glory of God
that is within us. It's not just in some of us;
it's in everyone.

And as we let our own light shine, we unconsciously
give other people permission to do the same.

As we are liberated from our own fear,
our presence automatically liberates others.

The True Leader's Creed

I am committed to being a True Leader

That's it from this day forward.
My choice is irreversible.
I fear not the unknown.
I will do whatever it takes.

I won't look back, let up, slow down, or back away.
I am finished and done with average living, small
planning, fruitless dreams, wishful thinking,
small talk, chintzy giving, and dwarfed goals.
I cannot be bought, compromised, detoured,
lured away, turned back, diluted, or delayed.

I will stand firm and hold my ground
in the face of sacrifice,
not hesitate in the presence of challenges,
not back down on the field of battle or
allow popularity to interfere with my purpose.

I will set the example, be the example and lead by
example. I will not look left, nor will I look right,
for I will always look up.

I will never settle for less than the best that I *am*.
My integrity and honesty will never be compromised.
I will be true to my own convictions,
whistle my own tune through my own lips
and march to the sound of my own drums.

I have committed to being . . . a True Leader.

~ Dr. Herb Oliver

Chapter 1

Insights from 21st Century True Leaders and Heroes for a New Millennium

Introduction

Art Burleigh and Jan Ruhe

IN THE FOLLOWING PAGES, YOU ARE GOING TO GET TAKE after take on *True Leadership*. We suggest that you get a yellow highlighter out and pay attention to all of this wisdom. It is from *True Leaders* who together have organizations totaling around two million people with over a billion dollars in sales! This is the only book with this many heavy hitters in one place giving you their collected wisdom on *True Leadership*.

It is with great honor and privilege that we celebrate having them all together in this one book.

Get ready to explode your own personal growth and development. Here it is ladies and gentlemen of the world . . . a great collection of wisdom by those who have been there, done that, been there, won that. We are thrilled to present all this magnificent wisdom from these *True Leaders*.

Special Thank You to Jim Rohn

Jan Ruhe

*T*HE *RICHEST MAN IN BABYLON* — THIS ONE LITTLE BOOK changed my life. Years and years ago, in one of the early seminars taught by Jim Rohn (one of my two mentors), Jim talked about and suggested that everyone invest in this book. There were at least 3,000 people in the room. He said, "I'm going to tell you all about this book. Only a few of you will actually go get it at the bookstore, and only one or two of you will read it, and only one of you will do what it says to do."

I decided right then and there to get the book, read it and do whatever it said. I am so glad I did. I did exactly what this book said and became a millionaire. Something to think about.

I had to wait until I was 35 to hear about this book. I was broke and had over $130,000 in debt from all the court costs and attorney's fees incurred to obtain custody of my children after my divorce. Although I made more money than most women in the world, 90% of it went to paying off my legal debts. I paid everyone back, and saved 10% first out of every one of my checks. Just like *The Richest Man in Babylon* book suggests. It made a huge difference.

I changed my economics after reading about keeping the flow of money going and not hoarding it—just saving some. There was so much contradiction in what I had heard and learned in the past. I began to save 10% of every check, pay off the credit cards and spend the rest. Enjoy it. Don't worry about the future. If you save 10% of your annual earnings, invest it wisely and don't touch it, that nest egg will grow. I promise.

Profits are better than wages. I cannot imagine working for someone else. Most employers figure out how to get the most work out of you for the least pay. Pay raises are hectic and can make you a nervous wreck, only for slightly higher wages. In Network Marketing, if you become a *True Leader* you can give yourself a pay raise by recruiting and selling and training.

If you constantly are a borrower, you are a servant to your lender. I hate to borrow even 25 cents from anyone. Be careful about constantly borrowing. Take personal responsibility for your economics. *True Leaders* have learned this.

It's a great honor that Jim Rohn has contributed to this book. Many people in this book have looked to him as a *True Leader* and thank him for his commitment to train, teach us and to guide us to becoming the best we can be. Countless thousands of people all over the world have been guided by Jim Rohn.

Jim, a special *thank you* for contributing to this book and especially to my life and the enriched lives of my children. Because of you, many of us are living the lifestyle of the rich and famous. Thank you, my friend! What an honor and privilege it is to call you my mentor. Because of you, I have a philosophy and the lifestyle you promised me all those years ago.

Qualities of Skillful Leadership

JIM ROHN

Iᴀ YOU WANT TO BE A LEADER WHO ATTRACTS QUALITY people, the key is to become a person of quality yourself. Leadership is the ability to attract someone to the gifts, skills, and opportunities you offer as an owner, manager and, parent. *I call leadership the great challenge of life.*

What's important in leadership is refining your skills. All great leaders keep working on themselves until they become effective. Here are some great specifics:

Learn to be strong but not impolite. It is an extra step you must take to become a powerful, capable leader with a wide range of reach. Some people mistake rudeness for strength. It's not even a good substitute.

Learn to be kind but not weak. We must not mistake weakness for kindness. Kindness isn't weak. Kindness is a type of strength. We must be kind enough to tell somebody the truth. We must be kind enough and considerate enough to lay it on the line. We must be kind enough to tell it like it is and not deal in delusion.

Learn to be bold but not a bully. It takes boldness to win the day. To build your influence, you've got to walk in front of your group. You've got to be willing to take the first arrow, tackle the first problem, and discover the first sign of trouble. I think we all agree that farming is not an easy job. Farmers must face the weeds and the rains and the bugs straight on.

Likewise, if you want any rewards at harvest time, you've got to be bold. You've got to seize the moment.

You must learn to be humble but not timid. You can't get to the high life by being timid. Some people mistake timidity for humility. But humility is a virtue; timidity is a disease. It's an affliction. It can be cured, but it is a problem.

Humility is almost a God-like word. A sense of awe. A sense of wonder. An awareness of the human soul and spirit. An understanding that there is something unique about the human drama versus the rest of life. *Humility is a grasp of the distance between us and the stars, yet having the feeling that we're part of the stars.*

Here's a good tip: **learn to be proud but not arrogant.** It takes pride to win the day. It takes pride to build your ambition. It takes pride in community. It takes pride in cause, in accomplishment. But the key to becoming a good leader is being proud without being arrogant. In fact, I believe the worst kind of arrogance is arrogance from ignorance. It's when you don't know that you don't know. Now that kind of arrogance is intolerable. If someone is smart and arrogant, we can tolerate that. But if someone is ignorant and arrogant, that's just too much to take.

The next step is learning to **develop humor without folly.** This is important for a leader. In leadership, we learn that it's okay to be witty, but not silly; funny, but not foolish.

Next, *deal in reality.* Deal in truth. Save yourself the agony. Just accept life like it is. Life is unique. Some people call it tragic, but I like to think it's unique. The whole drama of life is unique. It's fascinating.

Life is unique. Leadership is unique. The skills that work well for one leader may not work at all for another. But the fundamental skills of leadership can be adapted to work well for just about everyone at work, in the community, and at home.

Jim Rohn is America's foremost business philosopher. His career spans more than 35 years and has touched the lives of over three million people worldwide. He is internationally one of the most influential thinkers of our time. He has motivated an entire generation of personal development trainers. He's been described as a master motivator and a legend. He is Jan Ruhe's mentor and friend. Jan credits Jim Rohn with giving her the courage to go for greatness.

www.jimrohn.com
1-800-929-0434
In Dallas/Ft. Worth area: 1-972-401-1000 or Fax: 1-972-401-2003

Jim Rohn International
6311 N. O'Connor Blvd., Ste. 100
Irving, Texas 75039

Visit Jim's website and sign up for the FREE weekly Jim Rohn Ezine.

Special Thank You to Tom Hopkins

JAN RUHE

ATTENDING A TOM HOPKINS SEMINAR CHANGED MY life, forever. In the mid-1980s, I was a broke, tired, divorced single mother of three little children. I took all of my wedding gifts to a resale shop to buy a ticket to this seminar. There were 3,000 people in attendance! I was blown away! Excited! And *ready to learn!*

During this seminar I said good-bye to the old me and hello to the fabulous future that I would create for my children and myself. We would not be denied a fabulous future. *Lead me, follow me or get out of my way* became my mantra and philosophy. Some people get motivated for a few days— I got motivated for life.

Tom taught the audience all the responses that *True Leaders* use to close the sale, and that they all *need to have a personal growth and development program* and so much more. In the following years, I attended seven of his one-day events and became a serious student of Tom Hopkins' sales training. And, I began to read and lead.

I did *exactly* what Tom taught me. We had "Champion Network Experiences," where I taught my entire successline his information from a Network Marketing slant. People in my organization began getting results stacked on results. I ultimately sent over 500 people to his Boot Camps and sold thousands of dollars of his products to people all over the world. And today, we still use his techniques.

My organization and check exploded! I am Tom's number one female student in the world, have spoken at his Boot Camps, been on his special Showcase of Superstars, am quoted in his books and am now a personal friend.

Thank you, Tom, for being my mentor and confidant, for providing guidance, patience, friendship, encouraging notes and calls, and for your commitment to so many of us who thank you from around the world. Thank you for your contribution to this book, to all the *True Leaders* in the world.

❧ TOM HOPKINS ❧

Grasp the Essence of Leadership

——≈——

IN THE LATE 1990S, IT WAS A HIGHLIGHT OF MY LIFE TO share the seminar stage with some of the greatest *True Leaders* in current history through my association with the Peter Lowe International "Success" seminars. I've had the opportunity to meet and talk with people like Ret. General Colin Powell, Former First Lady Barbara Bush, Ret. General Norman Schwartzkopf, motivational legend and dear friend Zig Ziglar and Peter Lowe himself. I've tried hard to assume the role of student and learn as much as possible from our times together. The most powerful lessons I've learned have been about leadership and how those skills apply daily to not only business situations, but to our personal lives as well.

For example: General Schwartzkopf has a great definition of a leader that he shares. It goes like this:

"A great leader is an average individual who is extremely well-prepared when an incredible event occurs."

If you think about that definition, it tells us that anyone can become a great leader. After all, we're all pretty much average at the moment of birth, right? As babies, we have the same basic mentality and skill levels. It's what we do as we grow to prepare ourselves for life's great challenges that will make the difference in our leadership abilities.

Regardless of what you're doing in life, you're either leading or following at all times. As a parent, you lead your children. As a spouse, there are times when you take the lead and other times when you follow. As an employer, you lead your people. As an employee, you chose to follow the lead of the decision-makers at your company.

If you would like to be considered a great leader at some time in your life, you'll need to be well-prepared. But what is it that makes leaders different? I love to teach using acronyms, and so I have done this using the word leadership. Let me share it with you:

L   fall in *love* with what they do.

E   are *enthusiastic* about things.

A   have the right *attitude*. Attitude is everything when it comes to leadership.

D   have a *desire* to learn everything they can about their situation.

E   *emulate* other leaders who are greater than they are.

R   have the *respect* of the people who are following them.

S   enjoy the *success* leadership brings them.

H   are *humble* about their success—always willing to learn more.

I   have tremendous *imagination* to envision themselves in their next position of growth.

P   develop a burning *passion* for life, for what they do.

There are a few kinds of success that don't require *True Leadership*, a very few. Unless you're convinced that you'll never need to display leadership qualities, miss no opportunity to develop them.

What is the essence of *True Leadership*? The ability to make your followers believe that you possess superior knowledge of the situation, greater wisdom to cope with the unknown, or greater moral force. Unless you seem to have more of these things than the average follower does, they won't follow you around the first corner.

Superior knowledge of the specific situation you're involved with must be acquired on the scene. That's where your knowledge of how to learn will come into play.

Greater wisdom comes from study that's tested by experience. Although moral force is also a learned quality, it springs from an inner commitment to greatness that any of us can make. One of the best examples is an incident in the life of Alexander the Great.

Three hundred years before Christ, Alexander the Great led a forced march across a hot and desolate plain. On the eleventh day, he and all the soldiers who were still with him were near death from thirst. Still, Alexander pressed on. At midday, two scouts brought him what little water they had been able to find—it hardly filled the bottom of a helmet. Their throats burning, Alexander's men stood back and watched him enviously, knowing that as the leader, the first water rightly belonged to him. Alexander didn't hesitate. He turned the helmet over and poured the water on the hot sand at his feet. Then he said, "It's of no use for one to drink when many thirst." They desperately needed water—quantities of it—when Alexander had but a few drops. So he gave them the only thing he did have: *inspiration* to keep moving forward.

That's *True Leadership*.

Tom Hopkins is the number one sales trainer in the world. He is an author of several best-selling books and audiotapes. He is a master sales trainer and is recognized as the world's leading authority on selling techniques and salesmanship. Over three million people on five continents have attended Tom's live seminars. Tom personally conducts 75 seminars a year throughout the world. He is the author of *How to Master the Art of Selling*™ which has sold over 1.3 million copies worldwide. This book has been translated into 10 languages. He is the author of *Sales Closing for Dummies*™, and *Sales Prospecting for Dummies*™. Tom is a distinguished charter member of the National Speakers Association, has been the subject of countless articles in publications. Tom is one of Jan's two mentors and a friend. Jan credits Tom with being the number one teacher of her career. Jan Ruhe has been named one of Tom Hopkins' top students in the world and was an invited *Superstar of Selling* at the 1998 Tom Hopkins' Boot Camp.

www.tomhopkins.com
1-800-528-0446
7531 East 2nd Street, Box 1969
Scottsdale, Arizona 85252

❦ COREY AUGENSTEIN ❦

It All Boils Down to Personal Motivation

L EADERSHIP IS SIMPLY THE ACT OF GETTING OTHER PEOPLE to do what you want them to do over and over again. Here are the attributes of *True Leaders* that count the most:

True Leaders:
- **believe** in what they are doing.
- **instill faith.**
- **inspire loyalty and trust.**

True Leaders are:
- **articulate** and able to speak on a level that is clear and easy to understand.
- **able to communicate** with different levels of people relative to their intelligence and culture.
- **concerned about their appearance**—good looks can be an asset; looking as good as possible is smart.
- **good storytellers.**
- **confident**—even intimidating at times.
- **survivors.**
- fully aware of **how to use power**—some with very large egos can become power hungry.

True Leaders have:
- **total confidence** in themselves.
- **tolerance** with moderation.
- **patience** with moderation.

- ◆ **excellent knowledge** of their subject matter—or at least the ability to make people think they have that knowledge even if they don't yet.
- ◆ **a nice car.**
- ◆ **humility** with tolerance.
- ◆ **a sense of direction,** whether positive or negative.
- ◆ **strength of will.**
- ◆ **charisma.**
- ◆ **subtlety.**
- ◆ **awareness.**
- ◆ **strong egos.**

Some leaders use manipulation and corruption; while some are thrust innocently into leadership through changing or threatening circumstances, like the *Star Wars* movie hero Luke Skywalker.

True Leadership can manifest itself in a variety of ways. Most leaders end up being guided in the long run by their *personal motivation.*

Corey Augenstein is the Senior Editor of *NetWork Marketing Today/MLM Insider* magazine. He created the Network Marketing Millennium Leadership Cruise in the Caribbean which Art and Jan sailed on in the late 1990s. Corey lives in Florida.

coreya@bellsouth.net
1-305-947-5600

❧ CATHY BARBER ❧

Seek Out Information

───✦───

TRUE LEADERSHIP SUCCEEDS IN LIFE ONLY TO THE extent that you help others to succeed in their lives. When a *True Leader* is successful in helping others achieve *their* goals and dreams, ultimately the *team* is successful. This process begins with a leader and a team with a *joint vision* in mind.

Who is the leader is less important than whom you are leading. A *True Leader* first provides the vision and continues to learn about achieving and leading through building mystique—just like a magician. It's when someone seems to know something that we don't understand is when we are eager to learn.

> **"True Leaders make an emotional connection."**
>
> ~ Cathy Barber

True Leaders:
- **are not selfish.**
- **contribute** to the betterment of people.
- **do** the unexpected—out of the ordinary in unique ways.
- **don't wait for information**; they seek it out with a sense of urgency.
- **focus on others** and the importance of their growth and success.

- **go beyond** the average person's reach in continuous learning.
- **invest into the team** with a commitment to take them as far as they see themselves going *and then . . . take them further.*
- **keep pressing** into their inner self to bring the best effort out, not by building a fire under them but from within.
- **make emotional connections** through the team's growth and development.
- **take others** to the next step of success.
- **never hold back information**, but disperse it upon receipt.
- **put others' needs before theirs.** The larger vision you have will be met with this style. The words you speak, the recognition you give is unique and caring.
- **recognize potential leaders** who want to take on more responsibility and increase their learning, thus becoming a leader themselves.
- **take personal care** in bettering each person's life. Learn about them, study them, and find out what drives them.

Learning leads to new leaders. Leaders are out there waiting to be trained and taught. Deep down in every soul is a hidden impulse, desire and ambition to do something fine and enduring. No leader rises to the podium without the trust of others supporting the vision and joining the journey.

Cathy Barber is top leader in her Direct Selling company in Canada. She attended Jan's famous Aspen Nuts $ Bolts Symposium with Art in 1999 along with six of her key leaders. Cathy's organization doubled after Cathy sought out Jan to be her mentor. Cathy and her husband, Kris, live in Canada with their two children.

cbarber@idirect.com

MARILEE BIELSKI

Be A Sponge

FIND THE RIGHT KIND OF MENTOR OR *TRUE LEADER* AND become a "sponge" with a quest to learn everything you can by reading, listening and observing what they do.

True Leaders are:

- **busy** giving recognition. They see the good in people; they know how to make people feel important and appreciated.

- **consistently** learning, reading, attending conferences—always students. There is no such thing as too far or not enough time.

- **focused.** Nothing deters them from their dreams.

- **good communicators.** They realize that good communication is 80% listening and only 20% speaking.

- **happy** and upbeat; others want to be around them.

- **loyal.**

- **not afraid** to make mistakes, as long as they can learn from them.

- **persistent.**

- **risk takers,** create new ways of doing things.

- **teachers.**

- **coaches.**

- **mentors.**

- **want** their students to become better than they are.

- **write** the script of their life. They are dreamers, knowing that if they can dream it, *they can achieve it.*

True Leaders have:
- **affirmations** as an internal part of their daily lives.
- **systems,** programs and infrastructure, that enrich learning.
- **sustained** high levels of enthusiasm.

True Leaders know how to:
- **help** overcome challenges, with encouragement and resolutions.
- **prioritize** their life and to have *balance* between family and business.

True Leaders know the:
- **importance** and **value** of sensing when to step aside and allow someone else to lead.
- **value** of teamwork.

True Leaders:
- **act** "as if" they have already achieved their goals; *this becomes the fiber of their being.*
- **ask** themselves daily, *"Would I like 'me' as my Leader?"*
- **know** what their mission is.
- **know when** to let loose and let go, so the students can spread their wings and fly on their own—soaring out to be the best they can be, knowing that their *True Leader* will always be there to help and support as their cheerleader and coach.
- **lead** by example, so their team members are proud to say, "This is my Leader."
- **listen.**
- **realize** there is no "free lunch," and have to *pay a price to be successful.*
- **sacrifice** individually for the betterment of their team.
- **set** immediate, intermediate and long-range goals, knowing exactly *what* they want, *why* they want it and *when.*

- **surround** themselves with people who will *prosper* them.
- **do** whatever it takes to get the job *done.* Goals are written and read daily.
- **have** a "To Do List."

Marilee Bielski and her husband, John, are Triple Diamond executives with Essentially Yours Industries (EYI). With over 25 years in Network Marketing, Marilee is a trainer for major company events and is an expert in skin care. She and John are major leaders in Art's organization and live in Illinois.

Mbielski@ix.netcom.com

"ASPEN GROVES – An aspen grove is a single organism; each tree grows from a common set of roots. In the high country, an entire ridge can turn gold overnight! There is unstoppable, synergistic power and impact in teamwork. This takes time and planning to develop. Invest ongoing True Leadership in your team now, tomorrow, next month and next year—so it will grow in ability, reliability, stature and strength. The quality of your future may well depend on the quality of your team . . ."

~ Art Burleigh and Jan Ruhe

✺ RICHARD BROOKE ✺

Do The Right Thing

A *True Leader's* skill in dealing successfully with an infinite variety of people is of paramount importance— how we *act* and how we *react* to others. The challenge is twofold: developing and maintaining *our own* standards of excellence in our personality *and* dealing effectively with the ill effects *of others*.

Several defects in our personalities are not appreciated by others. Their *opposites* do, however, *endear* people to us. Developing and maintaining our own excellence means that we identify and choose to *leave behind* those habits we know tend to destroy our relationships with others *while adopting* those that build dynamic ones.

Although the habits on the left, in the upcoming chart, are often easier and more entertaining for us to employ, they can *only* lead us to a negative and lonely existence from which no successful leadership mission can grow. The right-column, correlating habits to *adopt*, however difficult to practice, *will always produce a healthy, positive self-image and an abundance of supportive, loyal relationships with others.* Obviously, the latter fosters growth in our leadership efforts.

How we respond to the unappreciated actions of others plays the second major role in how well we deal with people. When those habits to avoid are played out *on us,* we often assume that the person is an enemy of sorts creating *in us*

AVOID:	ADOPT:
Criticism	Praise
Selfishness	Giving
Jealousy	Appreciation
Complaining	Support
Distrust	Trust
Fault Finding	Accountability
Comparing	Self-Evaluation
Disrespect	Respect
Discouragement	Encouragement
Bias	Objectivity

emotional reactions of the same "ill will" (criticism for criticism, selfishness for selfishness, etc.).

By taking the time to objectively discover a person's *motives* for their attacks, we can act with a *productive* response and not *over* react. Examples of *harmless* motives are: ignorance, weakness, and a different truth.

Often the person is just trying to fill a deep void in their own life, or is simply operating on a different set of facts. Remember that each of us reacts in accordance with the truth, *as we perceive it*. So, our wrong actions are often just as right to us as wrong to others!

Once we clearly understand the basis of the once perceived act of "ill will," we can then design positive and productive *actions* rather than *reactions* that promote the problem. *Empathy is the objective.* For example: A person's criticism of us is an indication of poor self-esteem, a condition that can be repaired *with praise* (look back at the chart). We don't have to agree with a person's motivation, but it is appropriate to *understand* it.

Each of us lives in our own crystal cathedral. Stones can be the death of all our hopes and aspirations. Where people are so important to our success, we will want to protect and nurture ourselves by doing the same with others.

True Leaders have:
- a crystal clear **vision** that is circulated in written form.
- **empathy.** They seek to see things from another's point of view. They seek to understand how it looks, sounds and feels from someone else's vantage point.

True Leaders:
- are **continuously learning** new skills, new information and new technologies, so as to broaden the scope of their opinions and beliefs.
- call for **keen, courageous** and **unselfish judgment.**
- **do the right thing.** The leader must do what *honors* and *serves* others. This is distinguished often from what helps others, yet does not always serve them.
- **follow** when following is what the adventure calls for in the moment. All *True Leaders* have leaders of their own that may call on them to follow for a time.
- **lead** by example.
- **listen** to others with a *commitment* that others *be heard.* This is either a "clean slate" level of listening to clearly hear and feel what is so for the other person, or it is "generated listening" whereby the leader creates an opening for others to be empowered.
- **listen** to their supporters, their competitors and the world to hear what is missing.
- **perform** the tasks they ask others to perform—simply for modeling and training, or for leading production.

♦ **see the risks** and lead anyway, regardless of whether others cooperate.

> **"Vision provides Motivation**
> **Courage provides Inspiration**
> **Listening provides Honoring**
> **Empathy provides Empowerment**
> **Performing provides Training**
> **Learning provides Growth**
> **Following provides Humility**
> **Doing the Right Thing provides**
> **Secure Relationships"**

~ Richard B. Brooke

Richard Brooke started in Network Marketing in 1977 at age 22. He rose through 250,000 distributors to become the top trainer; earned over $1 million and became the Executive VP by age 30. He has served as a board member of the MLM International Association, on the Ethics Committee of the DSA, and is on the DSA Board of Directors. He was one of 10 people elected to the International Network Marketing Directory's inaugural Hall of Fame. He has been featured in several national publications. Richard is an *Upline®* Master. He is the author of *Mach II With Your Hair on Fire* and the co-author of *The New Entrepreneurs, Business Visionaries for the 21st Century.* Richard and his wife, Rishon, live in California and Idaho.

Richardb@oxyfreshww.com
1-888-665-8484

❧ DAVID BUTLER ❧

A Million-Dollar Example

M Y WIFE, COLLI, AND I WERE WITH A NETWORK Marketing company making several thousand dollars a month. From all indications our entire organization of several thousand people *thought* we were happy, but that wasn't the case at all. We were frustrated, our income had stopped growing, and our dropout rate was high. There was a lack of vision with the *leadership* in the company. We knew it would never be the kind of company we wanted to spend our career in. We were "prime prospects for a new home."

Within a week of each other I received two calls from two very different people representing the same company. We had never met either individual. They both "dripped" on us from time to time, sending us information about their opportunity. They both caught me at the "right time."

The first call was from Sam. He hyped the company to a staggering proportion. Biggest this, best that. I wanted to get him off the phone so I asked him to send me some literature.

The next call was from Mike. This call was wonderfully different. He asked how I was doing, about my family and about my present direction in Network Marketing. He asked permission to tell me *his* story. I listened intently. I asked questions. I heard good, knowledgeable answers. Then I asked him to send me literature.

Soon I had literature from both callers. Sam sent me a few

pages of seventh generation copies of something that looked like it had been pulled off the company fax-on-demand. Mike sent me a copy of the product label, a copy of their pay plan, and a book that was written by the product formulator of this company. He hand recorded an audiocassette tape telling his story, the company story, and why he thought it would become a billion-dollar giant.

They both followed up with me, but even their follow-up calls were different. Sam started up again with the hype. He told me about his past failures in Network Marketing. I asked him to explain the pay plan. He told me that he didn't like to explain every little detail about the pay plan, but it was fair, achievable for the part-timer and full-timer, and was the highest payout in the industry and if people worked at it they could make a fortune. I knew I wanted to join Sam's company. But I knew I didn't want to join under Sam.

Mike called and asked about my family again. I could feel him trying to build a relationship, and I liked it. Mike understood his product and his pay plan. He gave good answers to all of my questions, even my objections. I knew Mike was the one. I said, "Sign me up."

Now, four years later, let's look at Sam and Mike again. Sam is long gone. He is no longer with our company. Mike is one of the top three earners in our company and makes a five-figure monthly income. Over the past four years he's made a few million dollars *just* on the income he receives from Colli and me.

We follow the same *leadership* principles. *We build relationships* and protect them like we would a gold mine, for that is what they are worth. *True leaders* hardly need to recruit, for the dynamics of who they are and the principles they represent will attract people to them like metal clippings to a powerful magnet. Becoming a *True Leader* is a process. Develop a continuing awareness of who you are, the way you speak to others, the way you listen, and begin that process now.

There is a pot of gold waiting when one day you are magically perceived as a *True Leader*.

David Butler and his wife, Colli, are the Number One distributors for Freelife. David was Art's Upline in 1994. Later they went in different directions. Jan and Art were with David and Colli on the Network Marketing Millennium Leadership cruise in 1999. They live in California.

www.powerplayers.com
1-888- PLAYERS

⌐⌐

"Occasionally, it's necessary for the True Leader to be unpredictable and inconsistent. If you are too predictable some people will take advantage of you."

~ Anonymous

⟨⟨ ROBERT BUTWIN ⟩⟩

Become a True Leader

SOME WOULD ARGUE THAT LEADERS ARE PEOPLE BLESSED with exceptional charisma and communication skills—that they have the power to charm the masses with their "golden tongue" and sugar-coated promises. While "leaders" like that do exist, they're not the *True Leaders* I'm speaking of today.

> **"True Leaders are like a tea bag.**
> **You never know what's inside until they**
> **get into hot water."**
> **~ Robert Butwin**

No matter what industry or life circumstance you're in, people naturally seek out leaders.
True Leaders:
- always **do** what's right.
- are 100% **dependable.**
- **cheer** their followers on and **encourage** them to be all that they desire.
- **do what's in their group's best interest** despite the consequence of their action.
- don't **see people** for what they are today; rather, they see them **for what they can become.**
- easily **recognize a person's potential.**
- exude **strength** in every decision they make and every battle they fight.

+ guide people **down the best path** for reaching their goals.
+ guide people **to a better existence.**
+ **help people** reach their full potential.
+ never have self-serving interests.
+ realize the **importance of togetherness,** honoring the idea that "you're only as strong as your weakest link."
+ **stand for what's right.**
+ **stick to their principles,** even in the face of adversity.
+ **make things happen** for the right reasons.

True Leaders have:
+ **confidence** in their decision-making abilities.
+ **consistency** with what they say and do.
+ great **character.**
+ the **foresight** to empower and strengthen their group in order to achieve all that they can.
+ the gift of **vision.**

If you don't yet think you're a natural born leader, don't worry. You *can* develop the necessary traits that will compel others to not only look up to you, but also to seek you out, recommend you to others, and follow you to greatness.

Like it or not, there's a direct correlation between character and a person's leadership abilities. Money, fame, power and glory can't sway a *True Leader* from the rightful and just path.

How can you become a leader in action? Simple. Develop your own personal code of ethics and live by it daily. Once people see that you truly live by your words, they'll naturally be drawn to you.

Always have a personal vision for your future and share that vision with others. Let people know how and where they fit into the big picture and how you can *all* get there *together.* Becoming a *True Leader* takes practice. Few people are born with innate leadership skills. But, if you want to excel in life and in your business, you need to become a *leader in action.* Develop your leadership skills today and become the *True Leader* of tomorrow!

Robert Butwin is an MLM consultant, author, columnist, and a trainer. He is the author of *Street Smart Networking* and has been a friend of Jan's for years. Robert was on the Network Marketing Millennium Leadership Cruise with Art and Jan. He and his wife, Bonnie, and two children live in California.

TheSolutionist@aol.com
1-707-537-1042 or Fax: 1-707-537-1087
1051 Slate Drive, Santa Rosa, CA 95405

"Watch your thoughts; they become words. Watch your words; they become actions. Watch your actions; they become habits. Watch your habits; they become character. Watch your character; it becomes your destiny."
~ Frank Outlaw

JERRY CLARK

Find Mentors to Model
Who Listen and Empower

***

**"He who thinketh he leadeth and hath no
one following him is only taking a walk."**
~ Chinese Proverb

JOHN MAXWELL SAYS, "LEADERSHIP IS THE ABILITY TO obtain followers." *True Leadership* is knowing what these "followers" want and encouraging them to do what it takes to get it. In other words, inspiring them to take action towards the realization of a desired outcome. The key word is *inspiring*— not forcing, coercing, manipulating or tricking.

In 1992, I got to what I call a "Stuck Point." I felt like I was pushed against a wall and didn't know what to do to break through. This is when I decided to use a technique called modeling that I had learned from Tony Robbins years earlier. Modeling simply means finding someone who's getting the type of results you desire and then thinking what *they* think and doing what *they* do. Tom Schreiter was first on my list, so I decided to give him a call.

During our first conversation on the phone, I explained to him my situation and asked if I could buy all the training materials he had available. Instead of just selling me a bunch of stuff, he said he would like to meet with me since I was going to be in the area.

Insight #1: Be genuinely interested in the success of others.
Tom provided me with powerful information, giving me direction necessary to achieve my dreams, *and* he also left me with a bunch of his training materials free of charge.

Tom was seeing if I was sincere in taking the necessary actions to accomplish my desired outcome. This would let him know if it was worth his while to invest any more time in me.

Insight #2: Qualify potential "followers" for your time.
Listen carefully to what others say, and give them a chance to answer their own question. They will leave the conversation very empowered because since they came up with the answer; they will own it and feel more responsible for implementing it.

Insight #3: Give your "followers" an opportunity to reflect and come up with the answers to their own questions.
Serve as a mirror so that the questions the followers ask bounce off you and go to them so that they can answer these questions themselves.

Today I'm a millionaire.

Insight #4: Serve as a good example and give your "followers" a powerful set of beliefs and actions to model.
Follow these strategies, and you will be on your way to the top . . . Go, Go, Go!!!

Jerry Clark became a millionaire in his twenties. He is a speaker and the author of *The Magic of Colors, Creating Magic,* and *High Achievement Network Marketing.* His works are in many publications. He is the CEO & President of Club Rhino, Inc.; and the founder of AMG Business Group and The International Academy of Rhinology™.

Jan has worked with Jerry over the years and knows that he provides *True Leadership*.

www.clubrhino.net
1-817-595-6524
Club Rhino, Inc.
3020 Legacy, Suite 100-373, Plano, TX 75023

"Leaders can make a decision. If it's not the best decision, give it some time, let it alone and then make adjustments if necessary or go back to the compromise table. If you have people who are not willing to communicate with you, just know that they are not True Leaders and will be discovered as a False Leader sooner or later. A certain amount of opposition is a help, not a hindrance. Kites rise against the wind, not with it."

~ Art Burleigh and Jan Ruhe

⁊ᑤ MICHAEL S. CLOUSE ᒪᑤ

Build Relationships

WE DEPART KELOWNA AT 8:00 A.M.—A TOWN LOCATED somewhere along the 50th parallel in the heart of the Canadian Okanagan Valley. Long drive ahead of us. Have been told we are to travel by car over roads mostly of asphalt, sometimes gravel, and the occasional "you-have-got-to-be-kidding-me" dirt stretch destined to add a new rattle or two to even the most well-crafted vehicle.

Our final destination on this trip is Fort St. John, B.C., Canada. This is an area of wilderness the locals affectionately call "The Bush." With bags packed for our five-day excursion stacked neatly throughout the van, a full tank of gas, and music playing softly on the CD player, the journey, and our conversation begins . . .

We speak of philosophy, of life, and of its purpose. During the long drive, *we have a chance to do what so few in this world seem able to do—really connect as people.* We engage in endless dialogue, and by choice learn everything we possibly can about each other.

If the three most important things you will ever leave to your children are your photographs, your personal journals, and your library, what then is most prized when you are living? Quite simply, we believe that *nothing can be more valuable than your relationships.*

If you really want to *know* someone, you must *uncover* his or her *core values.* Here is how, by asking simple questions like, *"What is most important to you in life?"* *"What is important to you about that?"* *"How will you know when you have it?"*

Getting to know people for who they are is what we should do best. Sadly, as entrepreneurs we rarely develop our relationship skills as carefully as needed for that. *True Leaders*, make the time, and really get to know those in their lives for who they are, and for the individuals they wish to become. This is good for business. This is good for life.

"The next time you decide to develop a leader, begin your journey by becoming a friend."

~ Michael S. Clouse

Michael S. Clouse is Editor-in-Chief of *Nexera e-News* and former Editor-in-Chief of *Upline® Journal.* He's a graduate of the University of Illinois at Chicago and a Certified Network Marketing Professional. His books include *Future Choice, Building Your Empire, Seven Prospecting Secrets,* and *Business Is Booming!* Jan and Michael have been long-time peers and friends.

www.nexera.com
msc@nexera.com

❧ RITA DAVENPORT ❧

Love People – Not Money

TRUE LEADERS ARE:
- **aware** of the needs of others.
- **aware** that their rewards will be in direct proportion to the risks that they take.
- **committed.**
- **courageous.**
- **down to earth.** They know that they meet the same people going down that they meet going up.
- **guided** by their instincts.
- **loyal.**
- **people builders.**
- **responsible** for everyone that reports to them . . . the buck stops with them.
- **sensitive** to others.
- **willing to listen** to suggestions.

True Leaders give:
- credit to others.
- first and then receive later.
- something back in appreciation for their blessings.

True Leaders have:
- an **attitude** of gratitude.
- an **open door policy** to make everyone feel involved.
- **enthusiasm.**
- **high ethics.**

- the **ability** to make others aware of how each person's job is important to the success of the organization.
- the **capability** of influencing others to think and to act as well as to follow.

True Leaders know:
- **how to** use money and love people, not love money and use people.
- **they can get** the most from their team by not only seeing someone in their highest possibilities, but also by helping to raise the expectation of each person in their organization.
- **whatever** they do or say will come back to them.
- to **get,** you must give and know the importance of giving what you want to get.
- that **attitude** is crucial in every decision.

True Leaders:
- **are their own** best cheerleading squad.
- **believe** what goes around comes around.
- **build** confidence.
- **delegate** authority.
- **do not** take themselves seriously.
- **downplay** their own contribution.
- **find** people doing things right.
- **focus** on their mission.
- **live** in a fishbowl.
- **never waiver** from their principles.
- **promise** a lot and deliver more.
- **praise** in public and criticize in private.
- **share** their vision with only the few people that are knowledgeable, supportive and have the ability to be a visionary.
- **take** what they do seriously.
- take **personal responsibility.**

+ **use** their power wisely to build a team that has a mission that matters.

+ **work** together with others to overcome obstacles.

Calvin Lehwe, a good friend of mine, speaks about this in his speeches:

To create a mission, fulfill a goal or complete a vision, know these five functions:

1. Plan

2. Organize

3. Staff with the right people

4. Direct with instruction

5. Control the day-to-day results

Every person has an invisible sign that says: *"Make Me Feel Important."* Productivity improves when you find people doing things right and allow them to work in a morale-producing environment. People work harder for praises than they do for raises.

You can never be told enough that you are appreciated, respected, valued and admired. It's the same concept as the old saying, *"You need three hugs a day, just to keep from being weird."* There may be a lot of weird people in this world that are not getting three hugs a day, but often that's because *they* don't *give* them! You only get in life what you give. Praise goes up, just like it goes down! Most everyone has someone above them that, believe it or not, is just as hungry for praise and recognition.

Every time *True Leaders* open their mouths, money literally either goes in or out because of the way they treat others. Everything *True Leaders* say and do sends a message and sets an example.

Peter Drucker said that an organization begins to die the day it begins to run for the benefit of the insiders. For that reason, as President of Arbonne International, we do everything we can to make people realize, no matter what their position, they are an integral part of the desired results. People know that they matter and are appreciated. Imagine how a warehouse worker carefully picks and packs outgoing orders when they know that their photograph, along with a comment about how much they personally enjoy Arbonne's products, goes out with every order shipped. They have much more pride in the job they do because of the recognition they are receiving. This exposure makes them feel important. When someone feels important and valued, they are much more conscientious. Packing errors have dropped dramatically because there is much more ownership of the job. I love the slogan, "God is watching, give him a good show!"

Rita Davenport is President of Arbonne International. She is a keynote speaker, author, has been awarded the Certified Speaking Professional designation, has been honored by the National Speakers Association with their highest lifetime award, the Council of Peers Award for Excellence, and she was inducted into their Speaker Hall of Fame. Her books and tapes include *Making Time, Making Money* and *Programming the Power Within*. She is on *The Women's Tapes* and is a long-time friend of Jan's.

Ritadavenport@uswest.net
1-480-991-2990 or Fax 1-480-905-1084

❧ GARY DeRITTER ❧

The Value of True Leadership

Is ANYONE REALLY WORTH $25,000 PER MONTH? $50,000 per month? $75,000 per month? More than $100,000 per month? In Network Marketing? The answer, of course is absolutely! So why does a company pay that kind of money? It's *leadership*. So if leadership is that valuable shouldn't everyone spend time learning more about how to become a better leader? We think so. From the last ten years of experience here are some observations on leadership:

True Leaders:
 - **are always working on themselves.** Jim Rohn made an impression on me years ago when I heard him say:

> **"For things to get better,**
> **you've got to get better."**
> **~ Jim Rohn**

Success is dynamic, and *True Leaders* must always be changing, experiencing, learning and improving to avoid stagnation and obsolescence. The very process of self-improvement expands vision and belief by increasing potential.

True Leaders:
 - **begin with being a good follower.** Since the ability to keep it simple and easy to duplicate is so fundamental to our industry, the discipline of following and learning a system sets an example for others to follow.

It may be a challenge to leave out of the equation certain skills, habits and techniques that have worked in the past or in traditional marketing—but these same skills, habits and techniques would complicate the new system you're learning. Good followers often become *True Leaders* simply because of their commitment to a system.

♦ **believe in others.** It's not that they blindly believe that anyone can do anything; but rather that anyone with desire and guidance can do something . . . can achieve the next step and then build from there. It is that belief in others—often when those others don't believe in themselves—that inspires action and creates success.

♦ **have strong beliefs.** Leaders believe in themselves. This helps them act with confidence and with a certain surety that inspires.

♦ **have vision.** There are two parts to this. First, leaders have a vision of where they want to go, what it will be like and what it will take to get there. Second, *True Leaders* have a unique ability to share the vision in such a way that it attracts people to the goal, to the cause and to the journey.

♦ **never stop working** on themselves.

♦ **recognize** the importance of relationships. What a joy it is to work with people you like to be with and to share, dream, and travel with them as you build and grow together. For years we've experienced what we call "power weeks" by traveling to an area where an emerging leader lives and working together in a very concentrated manner to help expand their business. With this kind of focus, the car becomes a classroom. Meals together help create connection and common ground. By meeting and spending time with families you get beyond business and create lasting relationships. Once you really understand people and their needs it becomes much easier to help people set and reach their worthwhile goals.

The value of this leadership is well documented in the marketplace. But more important than monetary rewards is what leaders become along the way. A world with *True Leaders* is a better place. And the best part is: *there's always room for more.*

Brothers, Gary & Ed DeRitter joined Body Wise International Inc. in 1990 and today have a large organization in the U.S. and Canada. Thirteen of their successline have earned at least $1 million (and as much as $4 million) in commissions. Gary and his wife, Laurel, live with their two children in California.

deritter@gte.net
www.teambodywise.com
1-800-965-0276

❧ RUSS DeVan ❧

Just Do It!

THERE ARE QUALITIES THAT DETERMINE WHETHER OR not someone is a leader. Ironically, being a leader has much less to do with what any individual is or does but rather with what "difference" their words and deeds make to others. The irony is that *True Leaders* don't really care and are not attached to what people think.

> ### "True Leaders live out
> ### what they are committed to."
> ### ~ Russ DeVan

Many people are seduced by the acknowledgment and recognition (not to mention the power and control) that leaders seem to attract and acquire. These are gifts bestowed by adamant followers in return for the contribution that *True Leaders* make. Others shun the responsibilities of leadership with the justification that they are ego-less, modest and have no desire for power, control or recognition.

Nothing is more nauseating than a powerful person acting humble. It is the epitome of arrogance. It is impossible for anyone to do great things without a strong sense of ego. Can you name one world-changing leader who had *no ego?* All right, maybe one, other than Him? Think of a U.S. president, religious leader, or athlete who is without a little bit *more* than great self-esteem? Gandhi, Mother Teresa, FDR or Eleanor Roosevelt, even Santa Claus—they *all* have large, healthy egos. And when the "contribution" becomes *about ego*, leadership doesn't work—as with Napoleon, Caesar, or your least favorite president.

True Leaders:

- **do it with charisma.** They do it to be remembered. They do it for the greater good and to make a contribution.
- **Just Do It!** They choose role models—by holding someone *else* as a leader then creating their *own* "model" based on embellishing their hero or heroine. So, carefully consider what the qualities are that you admire in someone else or that are special about yourself.
- **recognize** their shortcomings and supplement them by surrounding themselves with, and even marrying, powerful people.
- **study** being a good follower.
- when they **speak**, others listen and follow.

True Leaders are:

- **crystal clear** about what they are building and what they are committed to.
- **listened to and followed** by others when they speak.
- **team builders.**

True Leaders have:

- **character.**
- **charisma.**
- **compassion.**
- **control.**
- **persistence.**
- **vision.**

Ultimately it is *others* who decide who a *True Leader is*. And I say a leader with only "followers" is an army of one.

Russ DeVan is a coach, sales leader and trainer. He is the co-author and founder of Success By Design Institute Online, and he has been featured in *Working At Home* magazine. Russ lives with his wife, Karen, and their daughter in Arizona.

RNDSBD@aol.com

"Just as most issues are seldom black or white, so are most good solutions seldom black or white. Beware of the solution that requires one side to be totally the loser and the other side to be totally the winner. The reason there are two sides to begin with usually is because neither side has all the facts. When the wise mediator effects a compromise, he/she is not acting from political motivation. Rather, he/she is acting from a deep sense of respect for the whole truth. If you cannot get to the whole truth, make a decision. Do not sit on the fence."

~ Art Burleigh and Jan Ruhe

❦ CONNIE DUGAN ❧

Step Into Your Own Magnificence

MANY FEEL THAT *TRUE LEADERS* ARE ONLY BORN. WHAT I've seen, however, in my decade in Network Marketing, is that leaders can be developed. When leaders lead by example, they inspire others to emulate them. *True Leaders* can duplicate themselves.

True Leaders are:
- a **vital force** in the world.
- **financially free.** When you are freed of financial burden, you can contribute to the world on a much grander scale. This is not to be confused with grandiose materialism, rather, being financially free is simply a capacity to enjoy life with all its rewards—and to be able to give back to the causes and charities of your choice.

True Leaders:
- **do not let fear** stop them.
- **direct** and **facilitate change.**
- **experience** and **contribute** to others passionately.
- have a **desire** to leave behind a legacy that will have an impact in the world.
- identify their **passion, gifts** and **life purpose** and then go out in the world to **share** them.
- **inspire** others to **spend time in self-discovery** of *their* unique gifts.
- know they **have special gifts to share.**
- live a life of **no regrets.**

- **live life at 100%.**
- **make a commitment** to the ongoing process of their personal growth and development.
- **master the art of listening** and provide it generously for others. When people are heard, they feel honored and appreciated for who they are. By listening, we show people that their ideas and concerns truly matter.
- realize that this **ongoing process of excellence** leads to a truthful and authentic style where they can be trusted and respected.
- **take a stand** for excellence in themselves, as well as their organization.

True Leaders have:
- **abundance** in health, wealth and relationships.
- **a sense** of their destiny.

Imagine a world where *all* is possible, born out of the commitment to spread leadership on purpose. You have the magic wand in your hand. All it will take is the *courage* to step into your own magnificence. *I promise you there is nothing to lose, only great gifts to be gained.* I challenge you to become a *True Leader*. Share your gifts and make a difference in the world.

Connie Dugan is the top-performing woman in Oxyfresh Worldwide. She was named "Woman of Distinction" in the 1999 Global Home-Based Business Directory. She has co-founded an international business called The Heart of Business, and is a trainer, and a long-time friend of Jan's.

CRD28@aol.com
1-843-842-6577

❧ SUE duPREEZ ❧

Build Your Dreams

> "If you have built castles in the air, your work need not be lost, that is where they should be! Now put foundations under them!"
>
> ~ Henry David Thoreau

THAT'S EXACTLY WHAT A *TRUE LEADER* DOES . . . HELPS you to dream of castles in the air and then teaches you how to build the foundations under them!

True Leaders:

- **ask** themselves, "What can I learn from this mistake?"
- **always** have a great attitude!
- **display** and **live** the qualities of honesty, loyalty and integrity.
- **empower** others.
- **get** people to take ownership of the situation and the achievement.
- **give** you the **courage** to set goals, even if they're only small ones to start off with. Then, as you achieve these goals, you gain the self-confidence to set yourself bigger and better goals until eventually when you achieve them, you grow as a person and go on to achieve heights of success that you never dreamed were possible. That's how you get to build those castles in the air!! Jan Ruhe is such a leader, who has done that for me and for thousands of other people,

too. Read more about this in Jan Ruhe's book *Fire Up!*
My whole story is right there!

♦ **help** you create a vision and help you believe in yourself.

♦ **lead** by example.

♦ **make** mistakes. "It's okay to make mistakes . . . so long as you learn from your mistakes! It's when you keep making the *same* mistake over and over again . . . *that's* when you're just plain stupid!"

♦ **read** positive and inspirational material every single day. I believe that every leader listens to motivational tapes in their car every day, too (with some upbeat happy music in between!).

♦ **set** the example to everyone in their organization.

♦ **walk** the walk and don't just talk the talk of a leader.

♦ were also once, just beginners!

♦ **watch** out for **big challenges** because they are just **big opportunities** in disguise! When challenges appear, you can *react* negatively by throwing up your arms in despair *or* you can *respond* by staying calm and *looking for a solution*.

True Leaders have:

♦ a **great attitude** when they're confronted with a problem and see it merely as a "challenge."

♦ an uncanny ability to make people **do** the things they don't really want to do, and by *doing* them, they ultimately achieve success.

♦ **determination** to persevere when things go wrong. To keep on keeping on when everyone else has already given up. To try and find another way or another solution to the challenges each leader faces through the years. To have the belief that no matter how bad things are going at that moment, that there is *always hope!* There is always a rainbow after the storm. To know that when you come out of the storm you'll be a stronger and better leader than you ever were before!

"Every challenge really does have a solution."
~ Sue duPreez

A *True Leader* knows and believes that—and helps to find it!

"To lead others to do right is wonderful. To do right and then lead them is More wonderful . . . and harder!"
~ John Maxwell

Sue duPreez is founder of Exclusive Touch Accessories in South Africa. She was the number one distributor in South Africa for Tupperware for years. Sue and her husband, Peet, have four children and live in Pretoria, South Africa. As well, they own a private Game Park called Bahati Adventures in South Africa. Sue and Jan are close friends and cruised together with Art on the 1999 Network Marketing Millennium Leadership Cruise.

wdupreez@global.co.za.
+27-12-346-3009 or +27-12-811-0671

❧ TERESA EPPS ❧

You Get What You Give

~~~

ACH ONE OF US, REGARDLESS OF OUR POSITION IN LIFE, has the awesome responsibility of leadership. Parents provide leadership for their children, teachers for their students, ministers for their congregations, CEOs for their staff, and on and on. You are a leader whether you know it or not and whether you like it or not. Leadership is an awesome responsibility.

True Leaders are:
- an **inspiration**.
- **committed** to the growth and development of people.
- **committed**.
- **ethical**.
- **honest**.
- **leading** to the extent that *they* are growing. A leader cannot lead others past the point where they are themselves.
- **not afraid** of putting the other person first.
- **of service** to others.
- **trustworthy**.

True Leaders have:
- a **strong belief** in themselves as well as in the business they have chosen.
- **complete faith** and **trust** in their team to get the job done.
- **confidence**.
- strong **moral** convictions.

♦ the **ability** to transfer their vision to other people while inspiring them into action.

True Leaders focus:

♦ **attention** not on themselves but on their team.

♦ on **creating value** for others, either personally or professionally, and their return will be much more than you would have ever expected. It may not always be in the form of money. Sometimes the payoff is in the form of friendship, pride, self-esteem or just plain old good fun.

True Leaders:

♦ **do** whatever it takes to get the job **done**—no matter what.

♦ **enjoy** making a positive difference in people's lives.

♦ **improve** through reading and attending seminars.

♦ **influence** others to follow them and accomplish a purpose.

♦ **lead** by example.

♦ **never** ask someone to do something that they would not do themselves.

♦ **offer** support to those with whom they work.

♦ **refuse** to live a life of mediocrity.

♦ **set goals** for themselves and help others see the value in goal setting.

♦ **teach** others how to focus on progress, not perfection. Single daily action will do more for your leadership skills than anything else will. It's the little things that add up to the big things.

♦ **will** not be denied!

True Leadership is not the same thing as charisma or the ability to impress people. Everything *True Leaders* do or say sends a message, sets a tone or teaches people what to do or what not to do.

Belief validates and therefore makes you confident. When your heart and mind are committed, you can accomplish anything.

"The best leader is the one who has sense enough to pick good people to do what he wants done, and the self-restraint to keep from meddling with them while they do it."
~ President Theodore Roosevelt

Here is what you, the *True Leader* will get in return for your leadership: your team will trust you and will have total faith in you as their leader. *Remember, you always get what you give.*

Teresa Epps was named one of the top five home-based business owners of the year in Nashville, TN for 1998-99 by the National Association of Women Business Owners. She is a National VP with Arbonne International. She is a trainer and speaker. Teresa is a long-time friend of Jan's.

Eagle85385@aol.com
Fax: 1-615-646-8941

❧ PAM EVANS ☙

Build Leaders and Make Them Successful

T*RUE LEADERSHIP* IS THE ONLY KIND OF LEADERSHIP that works. It involves people. It's thrilling to think that others look up to you. As the leader goes, so does the team. A *True Leader* attracts great people. *True Leadership* must be for the benefit of the followers, not the enrichment of the leaders.

In my experience I have had the opportunity to work with a *True Leader,* Jan Ruhe. I have chosen to work closely and build a relationship with her. There are qualities that I have learned from Jan, and these qualities have made me a stronger leader. A *True Leader* inspires and motivates, rather than intimidates and manipulates.

True Leaders:
- **are the richest people** in the world when it comes to experience, laughter, hope and love.
- **expect** the best.
- **go** with the flow.
- **have a positive attitude.**
- **inspire** the best in others.
- **make big things** happen a little at a time.
- **must be** close enough to **relate** to others, but far enough ahead to **inspire** them.
- **navigate** around the obstacles.
- **never give up** and **won't let you give up** on your dreams.

- ◆ say "Yes" to **freedom** and **change**.
- ◆ **see** the beginning in every ending.
- ◆ take responsibility and **empower** their people.
- ◆ **take** their **dreams seriously**.
- ◆ **walk the talk.**

In my experience, one of the *best* parts of being a *True Leader* that has been rewarding to me has been the friendships I have made with others who are going for greatness. I have found that those who are building their organizations don't have time to talk about or gossip about others. We spend 100% of our time working on how we can improve the bottom line, how we can sponsor more people, improve our training, move more product, move up the compensation plan faster and how we can lead the field with integrity, loyalty, honesty and get team spirit to sky rocket!

I have found that Network Marketing is not hard, actually it is easy. *Just do it!* You just have to have a *desire* to set goals, have the *desire* to move up the compensation plan, feed your mind, read more books, listen to tapes and listen to those who are living the lifestyle you want. Just because someone gets a title doesn't mean they are a *True Leader.* You may have the ability to get to the top, but *it takes character to keep you there*. The highest compliment leaders can receive is the one that is given by the people who work with them. A leader takes people where they want to go. A *True Leader takes people where they don't necessarily want to go, but ought to be.* One of the greatest gifts leaders can give is the gift of *hope.*

Always look for your next three to five people who can develop into a leader! *True Leaders* build leaders and make them successful. Begin today. Why not you and why not now?

Pam Evans is a Gold Sales Director in Discovery Toys and was their 1997 Woman of the Year. Prior to Discovery Toys, Pam was an accountant in the corporate world. She has two young children, Allye and Jacob. She lives with her husband, Kevin, in Oklahoma. Pam has moved up the compensation plan faster than anyone in Discovery Toys, is at the top of Jan Ruhe's Diamond organization in the USA, and is a close friend of Jan's.

Toyfairy@aol.com
1-918-252-9209

"No one keeps up enthusiasm automatically. Enthusiasm must be nourished with new actions, new aspirations, new efforts, and new vision. It is one's own fault if his enthusiasm is gone; he has failed to feed it."

~ Papryus

❧ PATRICIA FRIPP ❧

Leadership Lessons from Everyday Heroes

Leaders get results through others. There are everyday heroes you've never heard of who may teach you almost as much as famous business writers. Why? Because these people have developed the *ability to discover* extraordinary employees—right under their noses. Is there a gold mine of creativity, innovation, and leadership in your midst? Most companies have one and don't know it. You may have such a worker right now and not be aware of it.

Patty Lake, one of my "everyday heroes," told me about a woman on her staff at Shell Services International who had worked in payroll for over twenty-five years. "In all that time," says Patty, "she had never received a promotion. She had never been recognized for her contributions or led a team or participated on a special project. She hadn't had a raise in several years. No one ever asked for her opinion or input. No one offered her training or development opportunities. No one had even bothered to find out if she enjoyed her job. And she was the lowest paid person in her job grade in the entire company. She had been given the lowest performance rating short of termination for many years. She didn't rock the boat. She just did her job and did not complain."

Fortunately, I didn't know any of this. When I started at

Shell, my manager agreed to let me give each employee a clean slate. I would not review past performance assessments nor listen to old gossip. Instead, I sat down with each staff member to find out about them and what they did. This nondescript woman, along with several others, expressed an interest in learning more about payroll and developing her skills and capabilities.

I took her at her word and arranged for her to participate in the local American Payroll Association (APA) chapter. She took the basic payroll seminar offered by the national APA, took computer-application classes, and attended the statewide conference. *She blossomed!*

Late in 1999, she led a project team for a customer's special needs project, a highly visible and very delicate undertaking. The outcome was phenomenal. She and her entire team were recognized and rewarded by the customer for their successful handling of the work. In addition, she is now leading end-user training on the newly implemented web-based time and attendance system. She regularly speaks out in team meetings and has many creative and useful ideas. And she is planning to take the CPP exam and studies for it every day.

When she got her performance review in 1999, she earned a significant raise and an incentive bonus. She cried and told me that *all she had ever needed was someone to believe in her.* I did and I do.

Such a simple story from a woman you have probably never heard of and will never meet, but Patty Lake's example of discovering and developing a leader right under our noses could change your life and your own results as a leader. Now it's up to you.

Patricia Fripp, CSP, CPAE is a speaker and executive speech coach. *Meetings and Conventions Magazine* calls Patricia "one of the country's 10 most electrifying speakers." She is the author of *Get What You Want! and Make It! So You Don't Have to Fake It.* She promotes herself as "a speaker for all reasons."

PFripp@aol.com and www.fripp.com
1-800-634-3035
1-415-753-6556
Fax 1-415-753-0914
527 Hugo St., San Francisco, CA 94122

"True Leadership is to serve others."
~ Jeff Roberti

⚜ RANDY GAGE ⚜

True Leaders Affect
Positive Personal Growth

IN LATE 1999, I SPENT A WEEK IN LOS ANGELES, INTER-viewing CEO candidates for a venture I'm involved in. In 95% of the cases, I was able to disqualify the person within one interview. The reason: weak leadership skills in the person we were considering.

Many of these people were in what would be considered leadership positions in the companies they work for now. They knew all the buzzwords: leading by example, developing teamwork, creating vision, delegation and values. They spoke of managing resources and leading people. Yet I really believe they didn't understand the real essence of leadership. Most people don't.

I believe that a *True Leader* is someone who is *capable of getting people to willingly do things they wouldn't ordinarily do.* They are able to do this by helping them believe in themselves and teaching them not what to think, but how to think.

In the military environment, a leader might inspire troops to get out of a foxhole and charge an enemy encampment. A leader in a Network Marketing organization might inspire someone to speak in front of a group for the first time, or they might cause a new distributor to buy a suit and tie for the first time. In a corporate environment, a leader may empower an employee to take immediate action to save an important account.

In each case, the person wouldn't normally want to do these actions, but they willingly do them. They exercise leadership qualities because of the leadership influence of the leader they follow.

This is possible because of the increase in belief and esteem they have achieved as a result of their exposure to a leader. That leader has done much more than demonstrate leadership skills and qualities—they have helped develop positive growth in the individuals they lead.

The old leadership model was to teach people what to think. In the military model, examples of this would be civilian massacres and the Third Reich. The belief was that you simply indoctrinate people what to think (and one of those thoughts was to never question authority). The examples above prove the dangers of this way of thinking.

The fact is, many people are actively looking to be shown what to think. They search the globe for gurus to follow and movements to join. The strong growth today of gangs, religions and cults is a manifestation of this. People watch SportsCenter to learn what they should think about their local quarterback, they listen to bombastic buffoons on talk-radio stations to know what to think about political issues, and they read the social columns so they can know who is hip, hot and trendy. The education system around the world is changing from institutions that used to teach people *how* to think, into places that present you with facts to memorize.

Yet, although this environment exists, *True Leaders* do not exploit it. They carefully choose the people they lead, and select only those who are interested in thinking for themselves. They create situations where people develop problem-solving skills—which fosters thought and builds their belief in themselves.

"True Leaders don't develop people's belief in the leader; they develop the followers' belief in themselves!"
~ Randy Gage

They foster growing confidence and esteem in those that follow them and help them think independently. This free-thinking and newfound self-confidence causes the follower to act in leadership ways of his or her own. Leaders beget more leaders—the real test of leadership.

Randy Gage is the Director of the Gage Research & Development Institute in Miami, Florida. Randy is the author of *How to Build a Money Making Machine* and several sets of best-selling audiotapes, including the *Crafting Your Vision* tapes that Jan is a speaker on. Randy is a personal friend of Art and Jan's. Randy and Jan are Upline Masters.

www.randygage.com
www.mlm-metro.com
Prime Concepts Group at 1-316-942-1111

𝒸𝒶 RAY GEBAUER ꙮ

Fraud in Leadership

T<small>RUE</small> L<small>EADERS</small>:

- **are a gift** to mankind.
- **empower** people to take action. Without a leader, nothing much happens.
- **alter** the course of history.
- **have** influence and power that can bring bad as easily as good—look at the leaders in the political and global scene; clearly some have been good and some have been bad.
- **influence.**
- **envision.**

Yet also, True Leaders:

- **can be susceptible** to believing or pretending they are more than they really are, and then they become a fraud. This can happen *even when* the motives are good. I have fallen into this trap myself. To help you avoid this pitfall, look at me as an example:

I confess that I was a fraud.

Why? Even though nothing had been said or written that was untrue, or misleading, and even though I had good intentions (to inspire and empower people), I *pretended* to be something that was false—accepting and taking credit that did not belong to me.

The danger in this for all of us is that it can happen *gradually,* without a conscious decision to pretend. I was not even remotely aware of this, until several people who had enough courage and compassion confronted me. They helped me to see that others now *perceived* me as being arrogant and self-promoting. This was shocking information. I felt misunderstood and didn't understand.

Being frequently held up as a *True Leader* who had accomplished something astounding, I was given far more credit than I ever deserved and foolishly *started to accept it.* People told me how great it was that my organization was so large and successful, and I said "thank you" instead of correcting their misperception. I started to treasure their praise and believed I had achieved a great accomplishment. Giving God credit for my success wasn't enough. I started to think that a lot of the credit really did belong to me and that I had, indeed, done something great.

Letting my success be known, I thought, would inspire others. Then I moved from passively accepting people's misperception to actively promoting myself as an example of success, thinking that this would inspire people to do the same, based on the idea that "If he could do it, I can too."

As a result, instead of empowering others with these actions, they actually had the opposite effect. I thought that telling someone I had 200,000+ in my downline, or that I was on a mission to make a difference for ten million people would inspire people, that it would help people believe in themselves and empower them to success.

Sometimes my self-promoting statements *had* the intended empowering impact. At other times, people were actually dis-empowered by my arrogance, when I took far more credit than I deserved. I was cluelessly disconnecting with people.

The truth is that *I didn't build* an organization of 200,000.

This is what really happened: *I recruited a few people*, some of whom were leaders, and they recruited some leaders, and *they* built it big.

I played a small role, doing exactly what everyone else does: sponsor and support. It's the *system* of Network Marketing that makes me look good.

I was like the farmer who takes full credit for his harvest. All he did was plant the seeds and care for them, but it was God, through the laws of nature and abundance, that produced the harvest. And in my case, I didn't even do all the planting (recruiting)—99.9% of all the associates in "my" downline were recruited by someone else.

My "greatness" was more in my *pride* than in my own actual *accomplishment.*

Today, when promoting myself as a *True Leader* having achieved something great, people are not empowered by that, because they don't yet see themselves as someone who can accomplish something great. Most people don't see themselves as leaders. So, when emphasizing the necessity to become a leader ("like me"), people tend to discount and disqualify themselves and not even try.

Now I renounce the fraud that was allowed to creep into my thinking. I refuse to take excessive or inappropriate credit. The people that really deserve the credit should get it. As a *True Leader*, my goal is to make my contributions in ways that support and empower people to be and do all they can.

We are all susceptible to the delusion of pride and arrogance, an inflated ego, and becoming a fraud (pretender) in some area of our life. Be aware. Watch out. It can be so subtle. It can sneak up on you, and then be totally invisible. If someone ever tries to help you see a blind spot, be grateful for their courage and compassion, and take an honest look at yourself through the mirror of their eyes. Let's not let any degree of pride or arrogance or an inflated ego ("Edging God Out") dilute or interfere with our effectiveness in helping people. There's too much at stake.

Ray Gebauer is a top distributor and earner in Mannatech. His successline is over 300,000 people. Ray is the author of *How To Cure Any Disease* and lives with his wife, Diana, in Washington.

starmakr@nwlink.com

"Outstanding leaders go out of their way to boost the self-esteem of their personnel. It is the key to performance improvement."

~ Anonymous

ᘏᑐᗢ DONNA M. GREEN ᗒᑎᗢ

Lead By Example

BUILD YOUR BUSINESS ON *PRINCIPLE*. FROM MY YEARS OF wisdom, *principle* is the rock on which I have built the foundation for my successful career. You can, too. Principle is:

> a fundamental truth, law, doctrine, or motivating force upon which others are based; a rule of conduct, especially of *right* conduct.

It's important to apply principle in our businesses. If our business is principle-based, we are going to have a long-term business. If it is not, then we must change what we are doing and add principle into our work and network it to our downline!

If we allow someone to: malign, harm or hurt someone else, front-end load, demean others, sponsor someone and then not support them, steal recruits or orders, or gossip we are not principle-based!

True Leaders:

- ✦ **are principle**-based.
- ✦ **have** principles and values. What this creates is a fabulous future! Principle is the glue that binds all things everlasting!
- ✦ **lead** by example. A so-called leader can have all of the training, strategies and systems in the world to give to their downline, but the example they set will be what's usually followed.

'Like attracts like!" If you are a person of principle, that's what you will get for a downline.

Principle creates a safe and secure environment, in which all distributors can work in harmony. It's called *"the spirit of the hive!"* There is a team spirit, knowing that each, with their own special talent, is not working on shifting sand, but on solid rock principle, where everyone flourishes—a win-win environment for each distributor!

How do I know when I am performing *"right principle action"* in my business? It's easy. Here is my formula:

> **"If your decision will harm you,**
> **stop and go no further.**
> **If it doesn't harm you, you can continue.**
> **If your decision will harm your loved**
> **ones, stop and go no further.**
> **If it won't harm your loved ones,**
> **you can continue.**
> **If your decision will harm life,**
> **you must stop and go no further!"**
> **~ Donna M. Green**

Today's networker has a real chance to have all of their dreams come true now. You, in Network Marketing, you *can* have your own home-based family business and a secure future—all based on principle and honor. Live principle, surround yourself always with "right action," and you will be attracted to your solid rock future, because, *True Leadership* has Come of Age!

Donna M. Green has been in Network Marketing for 36 years. She has been on many advisory and corporate boards. She is a keynote speaker, a Double Diamond Executive with Essentially Yours Industries, and a major leader in Art's organization. Donna lives in Texas.

cle@connecti.com

⌒

"If one advances confidently in the direction of his dreams, and endeavors to live the life which he has imagined, he will meet with success unexpected in common hours."

~ Henry David Thoreau

BURKE HEDGES

True Leaders Make True Leaders

LEADERS COME IN MANY DIFFERENT SHAPES AND SIZES, with many different leadership traits. There are leaders who refuse to be challenged, who believe their way is the right way, no matter what ideas or different points of view they are presented with. Then there are non-assertive type leaders who value harmony and fear confrontations. And the ones who choose to do all of the work themselves, trusting no one else to "get things done." Most people who fall into these categories won't be leaders for long.

True Leaders:

- **believe they can make a difference.**
- **create a sense of worthiness** in the people around them.
- **create strong, open lines of communication.**
- **gain the confidence** of their followers.
- **inspire others** with their own perseverance and persistence.
- are the ones **people choose to follow**, not ones they are forced to accept.
- **make themselves available**, no matter what their "rank" in the organization.
- **realize** that the final goal, the bottom line, cannot be realized without the loyalty, commitment and support from those assisting them in realizing their goals.

- **seek out** all of the qualities that will propel them into greatness, and they apply them to their lives every second of every day.
- **treat people as team players,** not as subordinates.

True Leaders have:

- **confidence** and are trustworthy. Confidence and trust go hand in hand. People can't trust you if you have no integrity, and people will not follow you if they can't trust you.
- **respect** for their people.
- unquestionable **integrity.**

True Leaders understand:

- **people are more inclined to get things done** and be enthusiastic about getting them done if they help people discover *what* to do instead of *telling* them what to do.
- **the importance of showing their appreciation** to those around them and those behind the scenes that have assisted in reaching a goal or finishing a project.

True Leaders are:

- an **inspiration.**
- **confident** and have the ability to make people feel as strongly about their cause as they do.
- **dedicated** and **determined.**
- **diplomatic.**
- **eager** to create change.
- great **listeners.**
- **innovative thinkers**, ready to take on this constantly changing world.
- **admired.**
- **made,** not born.
- **risk-takers.**
- **unafraid** of what may lie around the next bend.
- **willing to accept change.**

There is no letter 'I' in the word team. This is also an excellent motto for all *True Leaders* to adhere to!

"A True Leader is one who inspires and encourages others to become True Leaders themselves!"

~ Burke Hedges

Burke Hedges earned over $3 million in four different businesses by the age of 28. Today he oversees several fast-growing companies. He is the author of: *Who Stole the American Dream?*, *You Can't Steal Second with Your Foot on First!*, *You, Inc.*, *Copycat Marketing 101*, *Read and Grow Rich*, and *Dream-Biz.com.* He is a worldwide speaker on free enterprise. He lives in Florida.

intipub@gate.net

"People who keep hustling are in great demand in organizations."

~ Anonymous

❧ HILTON JOHNSON ❧

A Lesson in Leadership

> **"A leader is someone who can get others to accomplish things they didn't know they had the ability to accomplish."**
> ~ Hilton Johnson

I N 1962 (MY SECOND YEAR IN DIRECT SALES), I LEARNED A powerful leadership quality from my sales manager, Jim Johnson (no relation), that would affect my own leadership abilities and my income for the rest of my life.

I had been in sales for about eighteen months (averaging one or two sales a week) when I got real lucky and made five sales in a single week. The commission on five sales like that today would be comparable to earning about $2,500! Not bad for a seventeen-year-old kid with a ninth grade education. Before getting my check I mentally started spending the money while telling my friends and family how successful I was.

Before getting paid, word got around, eventually to me, that all five of my sales had cancelled. When I heard this I was absolutely devastated. Instead of getting a huge wad of money to spend and show off, I was not even going to get a paycheck! Everybody in the office was sympathizing with me. The more I thought about it, the more I hated the business for what it was . . . a cruel, unforgiving, insecure job that was unpredictable.

I walked into my manager's office to hear the bad news directly from him. I knew he would feel sorry for me, too. He didn't want to lose the one or two sales a week I was making. But I had already decided that I was going to quit. Nothing could save me. I wanted out.

The moment I sat down in his office I noticed he had a mean look on his face and this is basically what he said to me:

"Hilton, all five of your deals cancelled this week! That means you don't know your presentation, particularly the part on how to close properly. I make an override on each of your sales Hilton, and you cost me a lot of money this week. You also cost the company money because they lost those sales, too."

I was stupefied. I thought he was going to feel bad for me; instead, he was blaming the whole thing on me! He went on . . .

"I want you to get into that classroom and learn your presentation the right way. I want you to learn how to lock down your sales, and I don't ever want this to happen again. Is that understood?"

All of a sudden it hit me: *I* was the problem, not the business. Although I thought I knew my presentation pretty well, evidently, I didn't know it well enough. I began to see things in a different perspective. The thought of quitting never entered my mind from that moment on. I went back into the classroom and worked on my presentation, and you better believe, *I worked on that close.*

I got real good at closing the sale before leaving my customers. As a result, I never had any more cancellation problems. This saved me tens of thousands of dollars in lost commissions over the years. And more importantly, through my manager's "tough love" posture with me, he saved me from quitting the sales business. I didn't know it at the time, but what a *True Leader* he was for me at that critical moment in my sales career!

Over the years I became a good friend with Jim Johnson, and we've often talked about that moment. Yes, he actually *did* feel sorry for me, and *no*, he was not really concerned about the money he had lost on my sales. He didn't want me to leave the business for my *own* good. Feeling sorry for me would have compounded my negative thinking, and he was too smart to allow that to happen.

As I later entered into sales management, I used the tough love approach on my sales staff as well. I learned how to do it in a very diplomatic way that didn't belittle the sales associate but at the same time, forced him/her to accept responsibility for himself/herself. I've had many salespeople who later went on to greatness come back and thank me for not feeling sorry for them when they were down and out.

Recently, some of my friends in Network Marketing and I got together during several conference calls to make a list of leadership qualities we could identify. We came up with over 40. You already know what they are: character, integrity, lead by example, vision, the ability to delegate and instill hope, be a great teacher, self-confidence, create a fun environment, and so on. But the one leadership quality that stands out in my mind is the one where . . . in a crucial moment, instead of pitying your sales associate, you diplomatically get them to *take responsibility* for what happens to them.

Hilton Johnson and his wife, Lisa, live in Florida. They have created MLM University with both online and teleclass curriculum. Art has been a student in Hilton's *Elite Millionaire's Club* division of MLM University since 1998. Art, Jan, Hilton and Lisa were together on the 1999 Network Marketing Millennium Leadership Cruise. Jan and Art are professors in the MLM University.

www.mlmu.com
1-954-491-8996

"I could not tread these perilous paths in safety, if I did not keep a saving sense of humor."

~ Anonymous

FRANK KEEFER

You Must Become a Leader

I HAVE SPENT THE BETTER PART OF MY LIFE AS A SERIOUS student of leadership. I've found that you will never maximize your potential as a follower. To make your life count for something, sooner or later, whether you want to or not, you must become a leader.

Most folks confuse management with leadership. The two may overlap, and sometimes appear to be one and the same, but they are actually different animals. Management generally involves a specific set of systems to achieve a desired goal.

True Leaders:

- are **role models** that the people want to become.
- are **attitudinal.**
- **develop the skills** to be a good follower.
- **inspire** (not motivate) others to operate in a manner congruent with their goals or their higher purpose.
- **place** high value on helping others succeed.
- **search** to find and **subordinate themselves to mentors** who will show them the way to the next level.
- **seek to be followers** to better understand how to be *True Leaders*.
- **set the example.**
- **teach** through example.
- **understand** their own strengths and weaknesses.

True Leaders have:
- **a personal mission.**
- **a moral code.** There is a reason why it's taught at service academies that a cadet or midshipman doesn't lie, cheat or steal or tolerate those who do. The academies recognize that without honor, one can never become a *True Leader.* Even the most cunning of moral eunuchs will be found out in time.
- **confidence** that by taking care of the troops first, before themselves, their mission will be successful, their goals realized.
- **courage** to do the right thing.
- **experience.**
- **higher standards** than their followers.
- **insight.**
- **mindset.**
- **personal accountability** and **posture.**
- **vision.**

Someone once told me that the definition of a leader is the number of followers created. I disagree. The number of *other leaders created* is the barometer of *True Leadership.* The greater the leader, the greater the number of leaders created.

Leadership development is a continuing process of trial and error. *True Leadership* is almost a lost art today. The bona fides of a *True Leader* are reflected in the obsession and desire of the people to emulate their leader.

While our citizenry may currently be intoxicated with good economic times, the fact that I have yet to hear a single person say that they want to be like Bill Clinton speaks volumes. A leader who allows his situation to be compromised by the trappings of power and prestige is not a *True Leader* and has lost the potential to maximize greatness. Honor is the foundation of leadership. Because success or failure is dependent upon leadership, honor, or the lack of it, is the ingredient behind the end result.

> **"What limits success is lack of leadership. What limits leadership is lack of character. The greater the leader, the greater the number of leaders created."**
> **~ Frank Keefer**

Are you a *True Leader*? Do you act in good faith towards others without reservation? Is your word your bond? Do you hold yourself and others to a moral code, or do you find justification or rationale to excuse yourself or others for irresponsibility? Do you make decisions based on self-interest or do you place the interests of the team goals and others first? I encourage you to seriously think about these questions. *True Leaders* do.

Frank Keefer's leadership skills have been recognized internationally. He is a former Fortune Fifty corporate executive, and is the founder of *Network Marketing Lifestyles Magazine*, the number one start up publication in North America in 1999, where he serves as President/CEO. He is one of only a very few who were awarded a direct commission for combat leadership in Vietnam. Frank and Jan have been *Upline®* Masters together. Frank and his wife, Gingie, live in Maryland.

frank@upline.com
1-410-827-5791
Fax 1-410-827-3972.

ᙍ JACK KELLEY ᙌ

Profile of a True Leader

TRUE LEADERS:

- **allow people to succeed.**
- are **enthusiastic.**
- **don't fear** their job. Some leaders have used fear as the driving force behind their success. My guess is these people enjoyed the power that fear brought and were extremely happy in their jobs.
- **enjoy** the job.
- **know** their employees and **what makes up their lives** which leads to more **team quality** in the work place. If you know what makes them happy after hours, the more ammunition you have to make them **succeed at the office.**
- **let people make mistakes.** That's the only way children learn, and the same is true for adults. This is one way to develop your people.
- **love** the job.
- **practice proper human behavior** to good business acumen. My approach is more toward the human side and where my comments are directed.
- **respect people** and their **time.** This is as important as paying attention and listening to what they are saying.
- **show concern** for their fellow associates.
- **show a genuine affection** for the position. When this is combined with enthusiasm, you go a long way towards winning people over to your point of view. You do not have to be a cheerleader type to pull this

off—just have a demonstrated enjoyment and sincerity for the position you hold.

♦ **think** outside the box. Have you heard the expression, "He/she is no Einstein"? I am not talking about sheer intellect here. The *True Leader* has an intellect to do one thing: think outside the box.

♦ **use good manners.**

True Leaders have:

♦ **compassion** for employees and co-workers.

♦ **influence** over others. This could be anyone who is in charge of people or has the financial resources to command attention.

♦ the **vision** to succeed.

Jack Kelley was a highly respected VP for a Fortune 500 company and has 30 years of experience in many styles of leadership. He is now President of JBK Telecommunications Consulting. Jack and his wife, Sheila, live in Indiana with their daughter. He is Jan's first cousin. They met after both of their fathers had passed away. They are very dear friends.

1-765-288-9470

"Our greatest glory is not in never failing, but in rising every time we fail."
~ Confucius

❧ PRIEST KEMPER ❧

Go Forth and Lead

T<small>RUE</small> L<small>EADERS</small>:

♦ are **aware** of technology and trends. They acquire, learn and use the powerful business-building tools: computers, the Internet, e-mail, fax machines and voice mail.

♦ **believe** in the product, company, industry and in themselves!

♦ **build** their reputation. Be proud ten years from now for the actions you take today!

♦ **communicate.** Practice and facilitate good communication skills with your leaders and distributors.

♦ **don't** get lazy. If you want your business to grow quickly or strongly, don't get lazy.

♦ **duplicate** their efforts to leverage time and skills, so that they don't have to do the work alone.

♦ **give** recognition. In Network Marketing we don't pay our leaders and top producers directly—the company does. We can only show our appreciation of their achievements by much-needed recognition. Entrepreneurs thrive on recognition, and they're usually starved for it. It's vital to success.

♦ **follow up.** Follow up systematically on virtually every step of the building process.

♦ **persevere.** Make phone calls and presentations until you just can't make another, then make more phone calls and presentations!

♦ **set goals.** Short, moderate, and long-term goals should be written down, reviewed and updated regularly.

- **stay hungry** for learning and always remain students.
- **support the team** and build relationships. T.E.A.M. = Together Everyone Achieves More.

True Leaders have:

- a **Buddy** system. New people need a buddy to show them the ropes by *doing,* not by telling!
- an **action** plan. Action makes goals and vision actually happen. Proven duplicable systems have fueled the success of the franchise industry and clearly show that moderate action that is consistent, is far better over time, than the inconsistent spurts of unpredictable stop-and-start action.
- **integrity** and **trust.** Integrity must rule as the confidence builder to give people the hope to get started and also the hope and "faith" *to keep on keeping on.* Honesty must prevail.
- **vision.** Keep a clear vision of time and financial freedoms, and other lifestyle goals.

"It's not your job to know where the harvest will come from; it's only your job to plant the seeds."
~ Priest Kemper

Beyond all of the commissions, income, royalties, traveling, awards, recognition, and accomplishments, the most grand of all meaningful rewards will be the lifelong relationships you will build with friends and loved ones.

"So . . . True Leaders . . . go forth and network.
True Leaders . . . go forth and lead!"
~ Priest Kemper

Priest Kemper is a Double Diamond Executive with Essentially Yours Industries. He is a major leader in Art's organization. Priest and his wife, Pat, live in Texas.

ppkemper@pdq.net

"Three people were laying brick.

The first was asked, "What are you doing?"

"Laying some brick."

The second was asked, "What are you working for?"

"Five dollars a day."

The third was asked, "What are you doing?"

"I am helping to build a great Cathedral."
Which person are *you*?"

~ Charles Schwab

ROBERT LOVELL

Managers vs. Leaders

O

NE OF THE MAJOR CHALLENGES IN BUSINESS TODAY IS that businesses are over-managed and under-led. The same can be said for any organization, including the family. If in fact this is true, it begs the question, "What is the difference between *True Leaders* and managers?" The difference is best explained by defining the difference between shepherds and sheepherders. *Shepherds walk in front* of their flock with the sheep following; while a *sheepherder drives from behind,* requiring the help of dogs, snipping at the sheep's hind legs to keep them together and moving forward.

One offers choice; the other incorporates force.

Both *True Leaders* and managers wield power. The *True Leader* has the power to influence, which allows people the right to exercise free choice. The manager has the power to control, which *limits* free choice. *True Leaders* tend to be innovators who simplify. Managers tend to be bureaucrats who complicate.

Both leadership and management skills are important. The proper balance between the two is required in every person to become effective in life. We have an overabundance of management in our society.

True Leaders are:

♦ **compassionate** and **give value** to all individuals.
♦ **decisive** and learn to **love change.**

- **driven** by meaningful, **crystal clear missions.**
- **ethical,** which cultivates **trust** and **loyalty.**
- **proactive,** not reactive.
- **risk-takers** and encourage their followers to take risks.

True Leaders:

- **accept responsibility** and do not fear the mantle of leadership.
- **allow** followers to **experience not only success but also failure.**
- **coach, cheer,** and **support** followers.
- **empower** others to reach their potential.
- **expand the vision** of their followers.
- **lead** first by example and then by teaching.
- **move** forward boldly with **great passion** and invite others to follow.
- **see** potential in all circumstances.
- **serve** their followers. Lao-tse said, "A leader is one who serves." A self-serving leader will ultimately fail.
- **teach** correct principles and let those who follow govern themselves.
- **think** "Big Picture."
- **treat** followers as **friends** and **spend time** with them.

Never buy into that great, destructive myth that leaders are born not made. Every person has the ability to develop leadership skills. Effective development of leadership skills begins by being a good follower. As a follower, it is extremely important that you select the best leader to follow.

To start your journey of becoming a *True Leader,* just figure out what you want and then *give it to others.* If you want friends, *be a friend* to others. If you want to be respected, *respect* others. Our thoughts, our attitudes and our deeds attract in kind, multiplied. *Live the Golden Rule*, and you will be well on your way to mastering the skills of *True Leadership*.

Robert Lovell has been in Network Marketing for over 35 years. He and his wife, Carol, have over 100,000 distributors doing in excess of $10 million in sales monthly. He is cofounder of Empower Net, a Network Marketing company. Robert created the audiotape program *Dreams, Goals and Achievement*. He and his wife live in Arizona.

robert@empowernet.com
1-480-964-4443

"The price of greatness is responsibility."
~ Winston Churchill

❦ CLAES LUNDSTRÖM ❧

Look for the Good in Others

HAVE YOU BECOME WHO YOU COULD BE? MOST PEOPLE think they have. They have limited themselves to stop where they are, without any goals or dreams of becoming more.

This is where you come in, both in your own life but also in other people's lives. How many people do you meet every day? How many of these people have reached their full potential? I would say—none! Some people call themselves leaders. I like the word *developer* much better. A person who can develop people and move them further in all directions of their lives is, for me, a leader.

Developers:

- **affect** people to the better, make them **happier** and make their **lives better.**

- **are in control of their lives** instead of their lives being in control of them.

- **combine** people's qualities and what they do best to maximize the results.

- **have** the ability to **affect people's lives to the better.** All people are less than they can be. Even the most successful people can become better.

- **help** people to **achieve more, grow more,** and **get more recognition.**

- **look** for the **good in people.** Too many people are fault finders instead of searching for the hidden good qualities that everyone possesses.

- **strive** to become more than they are.
- **take** action.

You don't have to be financially successful to be a leader. Success is life quality, happiness and being around positive people.

Years ago I used to always do everything for everybody. It at least felt that way. There was only one person I didn't give enough to, and that was myself. How are you leading your life? We all know the people that have too little time each day. How is that possible? Do they have more or less time than you? If you want to be able to affect people's lives then *you must first of all take control of your own life.*

I challenge you to make a difference in your life and in other's lives as well. Remember to *smile* at the people you meet. You *control* your thoughts and thereby your life. Your attitude is your biggest asset and the most fantastic thing is that you can change it in a heartbeat. Do it and do it now. Live the life you want and deserve. It is your choice!

Claes Lundström was born in and lives in Sweden. At age 26, he has been in Network Marketing for 6 years. Art and Jan are both friends with Claes from *Upline*® Masters Seminars.

claes@quorum.nu or lundstrm@oden.se
Phone: +46706255955
Fax: +46706155955
Box 7075, 17007 Solna, Sweden

❧ RUBY MILLER LYMAN ❧

Lead by Example,
Judge by Results

THE TRUE LEADER MUST LEAD BY EXAMPLE AND JUDGE by results.

> **"It is not fair to ask of others what you are not willing to do yourself."**
> **~ Eleanor Roosevelt**

The *True Leader* goes the extra mile and takes the road less traveled. Success will come to the person who gives more than they receive. Leadership is using your God-given talents to help make a positive effect on other people's lives and lifestyles.

Coming from a family of 10 children, I remember my parents giving me great life-building principles of leadership. My father led me to believe I was the architect of my own future and that *whatever* I did in life, to do it my very best.

> **"Put your signature on every job that you do; it's your mark of excellence. Be proud of a job well done, it builds faith in your dreams, belief in yourself, trust from others, strong character and pride in your profession."**
> **~ Edward G. Nordenstrom**

My mother told me as I took my first real job:

"Look like a woman, act like a lady, but think like a man."
~ Ruby Nordenstrom

These values, instilled in me by my parents, have been pearls of wisdom:

- **God**—my rock of Gibraltar and my business partner.
- **Family**—my constant source of love, happiness and approval.
- **Work**—the catalyst of every great accomplishment in life, the balm for the soul and my source of supply.
- **Play**—the joy and rewards from my labors. A time of bonding and love that completes life.

These key values have served me well for over 48 years in the Network Marketing Industry—and what a thrilling journey it has been.

If you give a man a fish he will eat for a day. If you teach a man to fish he will eat for a lifetime! *True Leaders* teach their Associates *how* to be good fishers of people following these guidelines:

True Leaders:

- **are** their own **best customers** and are a **product of their products.**
- **create a definite plan.**
- **develop strong Team Leaders** by getting them on the fastest achievement track possible.
- **draw** their team to local meetings, training and major corporate events. What great on-the-job training this is!
- **give recognition** whenever possible. It is **contagious** and keeps **enthusiasm** high while building a strong team spirit in your organization.

* **never** miss a meeting and never go to a meeting alone.

* **send** out basic info packs to interested persons then follow up and follow through within 48 hours while interest is still high.

* **turn their car into a rolling university.** They play a tape whenever they get in the car.

* **learn** from the Masters who have tried and true techniques.

* **earn a "degree" in product and business development knowledge by studying the profession.** They read books, listen to audiotapes on product, the Industry and their business plan.

* use a **duplicable** system. If it is not duplicable—do not do it!

* **treat** their home-based business **like a business,** not a hobby.

* **dream big dreams and set definite goals.** What is your heart's greatest desire or need for you and/or your family? Just know that whatever the mind can conceive and believe, it will achieve. So start today!

* **commit** two to four years to **build a solid business** once, and **enjoy residual income for life.**

May your *every dream* and goal be achieved as you cut into a bigger slice of life! Come ride the high places with us in the new millennium as we enjoy this phenomenal, fun and lucrative Network Marketing industry!

Ruby Miller Lyman has been in Network Marketing since 1951! She is a Double Diamond Executive with Essentially Yours Industries and has opened up their markets in Thailand, Taiwan and the Philippines. Ruby has been profiled in many industry publications, and was inducted into the Hall of Fame in the *Global 2000 Home-Based Business Directory.* She is a top leader in Art's organization and lives in California.

miller.lyman@gte.net

⚜ JOHN DAVID MANN ⚜

True Leaders Hold the Vision

YOUR JOB AS A LEADER IS TO HOLD THE VISION FOR YOUR people. They rely on you to do that; it's the biggest job you have.

The apostle Paul penned an intriguing leadership concept: "Faith is the substance of hope, the evidence of things unseen." When people start out in this business, they *hope* it will work. But hope is not a sufficient force to keep them in the game long enough to get results.

The Greek word here translated "substance" is *hypostasis,* which literally means "standing under." (Look inside the English word "substance" and you'll find the same concept.) Your *stance* is where you stand, your thoughts and ideas, your wants and intentions—and your hopes. Faith is what exists behind or *under* your stance.

The biggest challenge to your growing organization is the constant current of emotional entropy swirling around your fledgling business builders. They are surrounded by doubts and fears—theirs and others'.

Virtually every prospect you meet is infected by a universal epidemic of low financial self-esteem. People are just *looking* for evidence that "this won't work." They have emblazoned on the inside of their foreheads the mantra, "That might work for you—but it'll *never* work for me!"

Those whirlpools of fear and skepticism that bathe your new person's psyche are what surrounds their stance—literally, their *circum*stance.

One of the most important leadership attributes you can bring to a prospect is your clarity about what you're offering. If you are apologetic or defensive, they won't "catch the vision" from you-they'll catch *your ambiguity* like the infectious disease it is.

New business builders often worry, "Am I being too pushy?" That's a legitimate concern-but an overrated one. Equally important, often *more* important, is this: Are you coming across as too vague or ambivalent? Prospects want to feel like you know what you're talking about. They want you to be sure. They *want* you to be in charge.

That's why immediate and consistent follow-through is so important. The moment you hang up the phone with a prospect, their sense of your faith, your vision, your *substance* starts to fade, eroded by the entropy of their circumstance.

Those are the two forces—your substance and their circumstance-that battle to win the war of influence over their stance, where they stand *vis a vis* your opportunity. Sponsoring is not an event, it's a process, one in which your substance and their circumstance, your confident vision and their environment of motivational hydrogen-death, play tug-of-war.

Some people look for all the world like they're ready to set the world on fire once you've signed them up. Don't believe it. Circumstances will serve as a continual drag on their confidence in the business. That's why an "information packet" or other stone-cold media won't do the job: they need *you.* You are the evidence of what they can't yet see. They need your unshakable substance; your faith.

They need *True Leadership*.

John David Mann has been in the Network Marketing industry for 15 years. He co-founded *Upline®* with John M. Fogg, served as Senior Editor, design director and "industry insider" columnist for seven years. He has grown a Network Marketing organization that has earned him over two million dollars, is a popular speaker, editor and author of numerous publications and has served as a national trainer and TV host. He is best known in the industry for his "Last Word" columns, which appeared in *Upline®* until he retired from *Upline®* in 1996. He is currently the Editor in Chief of *Network Marketing Lifestyles* magazine. He lives in Virginia and is a friend of Jan's.

jdmann@upline.com
Voice mail: 1-800-800-4541

"Compare yourself to the world's best performers in your industry, then set goals that exceed the best."
~ Tom Peters

❧ DAN McCORMICK ❧

People Matter to True Leaders

———✒———

STOP! BEFORE YOU BEGIN READING, I WANT TO MAKE sure your mind is clear of the world, career concerns, and other events of the day. I want you to focus completely on the words you are about to read. You must be mentally ready to ponder these words. I would recommend you read them often.

There are people in this world who seem to accomplish more in a day than most do in a week. There are people who were told they couldn't succeed or shouldn't even try, yet they did and they grabbed the brass ring. People from all walks of life, those with money and education and those without, have succeeded at what they have set out to do. Of these individuals, those who are happy and at peace with themselves, have allowed a certain principle to govern their lives that is timeless in its origin and irrefutable in its results.

Since the beginning of time, in every facet of life, the marketplace has always rewarded leadership. The root of leadership was taught divinely in the ancient wisdom literature. Mankind has taken many different directions in his attempt to be successful, however, one truth, above all others has passed the test of time. *True Leaders* love people. When an individual studies and attempts to internalize this learned character trait, he or she will experience a more profound change in their life than through the study of any other topic!

Ponder for a few moments on an occasion when stress was eating at you and you didn't treat someone in public with kindness, respect or empathy. It was, for the moment, all about you and your frustrations. You were late or you were tired or you were shouldering too many burdens. The results of this interaction were probably less than ideal and afterwards you may have felt troubled by your behavior. Now flip the coin and think of a time when you showed kindness, concern or true caring for another individual. Remember how your paradigm changed, how your heart felt full of compassion and empathy. Love was given, love was received, and *True Leadership* was practiced. Perhaps few witnessed the event, but a significant part of your conduct in your private life will be rewarded in your public life. The result was an increased respect and your odds of building a future relationship increased. If your encounter involved recruiting or selling then you did more for future business than just building a relationship; you built your residual income.

What I have found in my life is that *people matter*. The principle of unconditional love shown to those *you interact with* will bring you more happiness and success in your life then adhering to any other code of conduct. If you find your life is out of balance and you are not achieving the goals you have set, then try to focus on others and their well-being *rather than on your own*. You are capable of great things when you first reach out to others. I have found this principle to be true in every aspect of my business and personal life. **People matter!** Unconditional love ties together the fabric of our lives and makes us stronger as a whole. *True Leadership* and the success that comes from it, must begin with this principle.

Dan McCormick, along with his wife, surpassed his first one million dollars as a distributor for Herbalife when he was 22. Dan began building a new business in the early 1990s with Bodywise International. He became their number one distributor in less than three years. Dan has been both a VP of marketing and marketing consultant for several companies. He currently enjoys public speaking engagements, and he lives with his wife and four daughters in Nevada. Dan is a long-time friend of Jan's

1-949-589-8912

"The four-way test of the things we think, say or do:

Is it the truth?

Is it fair to all concerned?

Will it build good will and better relationships?

Will it be beneficial to all concerned?"

~ Rotary International Motto

❧ DR. HERB OLIVER ❧

All Leaders Are Not Artists

———

ARE LEADERS BORN? PEOPLE SAY: "LEADERS ARE BORN" or "He/She is a born leader." This could be said about all recognized leaders. If it is true that leaders are born, then how do you go out and find them? Why are they so few and hard to find? How will you know one when you see one?

Often leaders can not be recognized because of their camouflage. They are really everywhere, yet are not that easily seen. You see, it is like the statue of David. How did Michelangelo produce such a magnificent masterpiece? His answer was: "It wasn't that big a deal. David *was always in there* hidden by the marble. All I did was chip away the excess and polish him up."

We are all born leaders—yet some of us have never had an artist, a mentor, to chip away the outer shell and place the final polish on the leader revealed. There are many stories of where great athletes have become *great* because they were able to fall into the hands of a *great* coach. The same is true for so many musicians, students, children and painters.

It takes one to know one.

If this is true, then *a leader knows*.

To become a leader requires that you do it yourself and yet know that you can't do it alone. Find a mentor, a

Michelangelo, to chip away the outer covering and expose what has been inside all the time.

To begin with "You Gotta Wanna," and to get there, *you must change.*

If you continue to do the things you've always done, you will continue to get the things you've got!

Leaders *act* in a certain way, because they *think* in a certain way. They know how to control their thinking. They *think by choice.* They are aware of their thoughts and choose which ones they let in. Good thoughts produce good results. The secret to getting different results is to know what you are thinking and to choose your thoughts carefully.

A *True Leader* knows that being a leader is a never-ending process of learning and becoming. It all starts with being. *Know* that you *are* a born leader. We all have dreams and aspirations. The makings of everything start from within. You already have everything you need. You can do everything you must do, and you already know everything there is to know.

For those who want to become a leader, go find yourself a leader, a mentor, *an artist*, and never stop looking till you find one. For those who want to find leaders, there are more seeking you for mentoring than you could serve in a lifetime. When looking for a leader, don't hold your breath waiting for the polished "Statue of David" to show up. You become a *True Leader*, an artist, then find yourself the right block of marble and start chipping away. That is what really makes the difference. All leaders are born and all leaders are not artists. A *True Leader* knows.

Dr. Herb Oliver is a Triple Diamond Executive for Essentially Yours Industries. He's a professional Network Marketing trainer. Herb is the father of two children, and he lives in Florida. He's a major leader in Art's organization.

holi1@tampabay.rr.com
1-727-517-8564

"The greatest contribution leaders can make to mankind is to use their power in a positive way, to help and inspire others."

~ Anonymous

ᨄᨆ DR. JOE RUBINO ᨆᨆ

Be The Source of Your Success

WHAT DOES IT REALLY MEAN TO BE A LEADER AND WHAT does it take to actually step into a leadership role?

Most people often wait until they have achieved a certain level of success in Network Marketing before they feel they have earned the right to step into a leadership role. Being a *True Leader* is not a position you acquire as a result of having achieved a certain volume or compensation plan position. It is a place you come from as a *declaration* that guides your decisions and actions. When you declare that you are the source of everything that shows up around you in your life and in your business, your actions will be in sync with your self-declared leadership role.

True Leaders:
- **empower** you through example with a commitment to seeing a possibility for you that you might not yet clearly see for yourself.
- **assume responsibility** for being the source of everything that shows up around them with an expectation that they can and will impact their world and bring about a desired result.
- **believe** and have the ability to **transfer their beliefs to others.**
- **care** about and **serve others.**
- have the **ability to make others greater** than themselves.

+ **inspire** others to be all that they can be and in the process make others great.

+ **set the pace** with unstoppable actions.

True Leaders are:

+ **creative** and will find a way to do whatever it takes to realize their goals while honoring their values. *Focused* action is the key. A vision without *action* is self-delusion.

+ **enthusiastic.** Their belief level causes others to join in the cause and get into action motivated by a positive expectation of success.

+ **visionaries** with the **courage to act.** A leader's vision always possesses an element of contribution to others. If the vision is only self-serving, it will inspire no one to follow.

True Leaders have:

+ a **commitment** to ultimate invisibility. This means eventually getting out of the way, allowing others to step into *their own power* as *they* in turn assume the prominence *you* once held.

+ a specific **action plan** that answers the question, "What exactly will it take to manifest this vision?"

+ an **authenticity** and **genuine humility** that comes from a true commitment to be of contribution to others.

Leadership is both the driving force that propels a Network Marketing organization and the glue that keeps it together long term, allowing it to withstand the inevitable challenges that will develop from time to time. Today, "do the right thing" leadership will be regarded as *the* most noble of professions. With the same power of geometric progression that causes Network Marketing companies to explode with success, inspirational charismatic leaders committed to the excellence and empowerment of people and the realization of noble principles will likewise spawn other leaders committed to more of the same. It is in this manner that our world will be impacted for the better with an ever-growing bumper crop of inspirational *True Leaders*.

Dr. Joe Rubino is a trainer, author and success coach. He is the author of *Secrets Of Building A Million-Dollar Network-Marketing Organization From A Guy Who's Been There Done That*, and *The Magic Lantern*. He is the cofounder of "Conversations For Success," a course in personal and productivity development. Joe is a top distributor for an international Network Marketing company. He is a friend of Jan's and lives in Massachusetts.

DrJRubino@email.com,
800-999-9551 Ext. 870
PO Box 217, Boxford, MA 01921
http://Come.to/ConversationsForSuccess.

⌒

"Good leadership consists of showing average people how to do the work of superior people."
~ John D. Rockefeller

⟊ TIM SALES ⟊

Teach a Man to Fish

LEADERSHIP TO ME IS VERY SIMPLE. TWO STEPS:

First, grab as much responsibility as you possibly can, to the point that it makes you want to quit every day, then—

don't quit!

Congratulations, *you* are a leader.

Lieutenant Mike Scott, an officer in the U.S. Navy Explosive Ordnance Disposal Team (the Navy's bomb squad) is to this day the most impressive leader I've ever had the privilege of working with. He probably has no idea of the impact he had on me. I am eternally blessed that I had the honor to work within his ranks.

Kahoolewe is a Hawaiian island that was used as a practice-bombing site since before World War II. Not just by U.S.-based military forces but also by several NATO forces too. There were literally thousands of unexploded bombs on the island. The military lost the rights to a portion of the island in a legal decision, which required them to clear the entire island of all unexploded bombs.

To this day I can still see the glimmer in Lt. Scott's eyes when he was volunteering us for the mission. He "worked" at ensuring that his team would be the team to get the job. At the time, I was a 22-year old young man, confused about why anyone would aggressively seek to get this job. Traditionally, if a bomb squad technician has to defuse one or two real bombs in his entire career, it's a *big deal*. They speak in terms of a four-leaf clover. Each time you work on a "real bomb," you tear one leaf off the clover. After the fourth bomb . . . you're "out of luck." The assignment of this mission would have us rendering safe five to ten bombs *a day!* Lt. Scott and his team got the mission of rendering safe *all* the bombs on Kahoolewe Island!

Lt. Scott's reputation was that he was impossible to work for because he loaded all of us down with so much responsibility that we all wanted to quit. Little did I know that the two short years that I would work for him would be *the best leadership training I would ever receive!*

I felt that this "about to choke" responsibility level was required to teach me *efficiencies* and *delegation*. I've never found a person to develop leadership qualities without first creating such a chaotic state that it drives them to get good at *teaching others*.

The second step of leadership is having the patience to train others. Have you ever heard people say, "It's quicker to just do it myself than to try to get others to do it?" Is it really? Or, "It's easier to do it myself than to get someone else to do it?" Is it? In business I say *wealth is hidden from those who must do it all themselves; wealth exposes itself to those patient enough to train others. People learn how to do the things you want them to when you learn the patience to teach them.*

Suppose you have a four-year-old son. His shoestrings are untied. You've got a choice. You can tie the shoes for him and it will be done "quicker." *Or* you can *teach him how*. If you've ever tried this you know he'll ignore you when you first try to teach him. By the way, he doesn't have an attention deficit.

Chances are higher that you have a teaching deficit. Try having *him* hold one of the strings while you tie around it. Keep doing that for two to three weeks and he'll be trying to get the other string out of your hand. When he finally does tie the knot himself, his knot won't hold. Keep teaching. After a couple of weeks, or even months he'll tie his own shoes—*for the rest of his life!*

Equally as important is that you'll have developed the patience to teach, you'll be more productive because he is now tying his own shoes, and more importantly you will have built a little guy with pride. The lesson doesn't stop here.

What if your leadership lesson wasn't complete until you properly trained your son to train *his sister* how to tie *her* shoes? That's duplication!

> **"Give a man a fish, he'll eat today.**
> **Teach a man to fish, he'll eat for a lifetime.**
> **Teach a man how to train his children—**
> **to train their children how to fish—**
> **and you'll end world hunger forever!"**

Tim Sales is the creator of the Brilliant Compensation® video and audio training tapes. Tim's organization is now in 20 countries. He is an industry speaker and trainer. Tim is a friend of Art's from the *Upline*® Lifers Retreat. Jan and Tim were speakers at the MLM Millennium Symposium in January 2000 in Los Angeles.

tim@brilliantcompensation.com

JAY SARGEANT

Ride the Bus

WHEN ESSENTIALLY YOURS WAS YOUNG, ONE OF MY leaders, who has given Network Marketing 35 full-time years, said, "You know the thing I like about you is that you ride the bus." He meant of course that when we have company events, my partners and I always ride with our EYI family on the bus.

I was stunned; I couldn't imagine another way. I said, "Where else would I ride?" He told me that in his three previous companies, the owners took private transportation. I laughed and said, "That sure doesn't sound like fun to me."

In truth, we ride the bus because it is fun, *it builds friendships*, it builds *deep loyalties* that help us forge through tough times, and most importantly . . . *that's* where we learn to serve our partners in the business—our distributors.

When we began our new company, it was a very hands-on operation for the partners. We did the sales presentations, wrote the newsletters, gave all the training, shipped the product, tracked orders, did the conference calls and handled customer service. Back then, we were personally in touch with *all elements,* so we always knew what to fix and when.

As we grew, my role changed and removed me from the direct front-line activities of retailing and recruiting. I discovered that I was no longer the best presenter, the best closer or the best recruiter in our business. The very "best" ride the bus, *and I listen.*

This is not a new concept in *True Leadership*. It goes back centuries. In the 1946 movie of Shakespeare's Henry V, Sir Lawrence Olivier gave a *classic* speech delivered by King Henry preceding the Battle of Agincourt (France, 1415).

The night before this key battle, King Henry, disguised by a hooded robe, wandered from warrior campfire to campfire. There, he heard his men heroically proclaim their allegiance to the death for England the next day. Nice sentiment, but not exactly an encouraging state of mind—if you are hoping to *win* the battle.

The next day, Henry delivered one of the greatest speeches in military history, rousing his small army to miraculous victory. Yet the speech is not as important as the *preparation* that created it. Henry delivered the perfect message *because he knew the mind, the mood and the heart of his troops.* The night before, he had gathered strategic information that allowed him to assess his men's strengths and weaknesses.

Henry chose to "ride the bus," and the payoff was delivering a powerful speech that leveraged the right criteria, creating a state of mind conducive to enormous pluck, courage and resolve. In that empowered state, his troops became invincible, and they achieved a stunning victory against huge odds and a *much* larger French army!

How do I prepare for my speeches? I model King Henry: I get my inspirations in the elevator, in the lobby and in the coffee shop of the hotel where our team is gathering. *I ask people questions. I find out what's working and what isn't.*

Millions of us long for a home, for a business that makes more than sense, for a business that *makes us whole*, that connects us to a goal, a shared experience of fellowship and freedom. If we truly want to give *True Leadership* to these core impulses and forge networks that break the mold and create new paths and paradigms in business, we must be *True Leaders in the trenches* not up on the hill.

The knowledge we *really* need will never be experienced in the isolation of the home office. *You only get this perspective on the bus.*

Jay Sargeant has led and trained sales forces since 1980. He authored *Paradigms of Persuasion* and has created training systems, tapes and tools for many companies. He is a founding partner with Essentially Yours Industries and launched their U.S. operations from his home in California.

eyi@mediaone.net

⌒

"Great leaders are never satisfied with current levels of performance. They constantly strive for higher and higher levels of achievement."

~ Anonymous

KRISTAN SARGEANT

Press On True Leaders

⌇

M Y DAD AND I THREW TOGETHER AN OFFICE SPACE over the garage in his backyard. And there we started Essentially Yours Industries (EYI) in the U.S. Our office was a mix of folding tables and patio furniture. In the garage, we established our shipping operation. On a good day, our *one* case of inventory, which constituted the entire U.S. stock, would get depleted.

It was slow going. When a potential customer showed up at the "Corporate Headquarters," they had to kind of carve out a space for themselves in the rubble of paperwork strewn all over the floor.

Our business began to sprout, and before we knew it FedEx was sending us custom company labels by the ream! People started to buy our products. From a shoebox operation with nothing more than third generation Xeroxed literature for sales aids, we started to grow . . . big time.

Things were really beginning to hop in the business. We had moved into a bigger office space at this time and brought on some additional staff. We had a hit product that was quickly reaching legendary status, but it was all new and extremely fragile.

One of my favorite employees was a treasure trove of amazing tales. It didn't matter if the stories were true or not, the telling of them was so charming and inspired. However, unfortunately, he was selling secrets to a competitive company that was trying to knock off our product. He was using *our* phone lines to turn every detail of our business inside out for his personal profit. It was my first real experience of betrayal. It had bite in it that made me stark raving angry.

That competitor of ours started gaining a little ground. They were putting out sabotaging information about us, turning the heads of some of our associates. I drove several hours to a meeting one night only to be greeted by a barrage of angry accusations.

I finally unloaded this unrest on my father. I was trembling with rage and sadness.

My father said this:

> **"God bless them. That's the beauty of free-market capitalism and democracy. Each person can go out and pursue what he believes is the best destiny for him. Furthermore, there's enough market share for all of us. If we've inspired someone to go out and create a product that actually helps people, more power to them. All we can do is stay true to our purpose and keep moving forward."**
>
> ~ Jay Sargeant, my dad

My dad taught me about *forgiveness, abundance and not letting anyone steal your reality*. Of course, that other company failed. However, through this experience my dad, a *True Leader,* taught me that valuable lesson. Pay attention. It's okay if you are disappointed. *True Leaders* press on.

Kristan Sargeant is a Triple Diamond Executive with Essentially Yours Industries, and is Art's Upline. Her organization moved over $144 million in wholesale products from 1996-2000. Kristan joined EYI when she was 22 years old. She's a Columbia University graduate, and she lives in California.

stan2@mediaone.net

⌒⌒

"True Leaders bring out the best in people by stimulating them to achieve what they thought was impossible."

~ Anonymous

⁂ TOM SCHREITER ⁂

True Leadership Test

A GROUP OF DISTRIBUTORS WAS SITTING AROUND HAVING coffee after a disappointing opportunity meeting. While complaining about their lack of downline activity, one distributor said, "Hey, you know what the real problem is? The company doesn't pay enough commissions on retail sales. That's what's causing my distributors to drop out."

"And you know what else my company should do?" added another distributor. "They should pay out a 50% bonus on our first levels so all of our distributors will make money sooner!"

"The company should also lower prices on its products. That way we could get more people to buy," said another.

"Distributors should earn more in bonuses than what they spend for products. And the company should give free products to prospective customers. We should just have to handle reorders."

The conversation grew heated as the rest of the distributors joined in with their solutions.

"We need more support from the company. The home office is just a bunch of order takers."

"There should be a 60% bonus paid on second level distributors to help our downlines make more money."

"They should make our sponsors recruit our downlines."

"Our downlines should have higher purchasing requirements. Then we could make more overrides."

"The company should telephone our inactive distributors. Also, they should send them free newsletters for a year, in case they might get interested again."

"The real problem is that the brochures aren't wide enough. My sponsor would give me free brochures if they were wider."

"Everyone should receive a monthly bonus check, even if they don't order. Then we would have real motivation in our groups. Buying products shouldn't be mandatory."

"My dropouts would decrease if the company paid a 70% bonus on the third level. And why should I spend money calling my downline? They can call me if they have problems."

"The rules should be different for me; I'm a leader."

Finally one distributor stood up. "It seems to me we're just trying to find a way not to work. If the company and our Upline did all the recruiting, selling, and motivating, why would they need us? Let's face the truth. *We are paid for producing results, not for finding ways for others to earn our money. Hey, if it was easy, everyone would be a leader.*"

After a stunned silence, one distributor said, "Whoa, it's getting late. I'm going to miss the sports report on the evening news. See you guys next week."

Another distributor said, "I got to go to work early tomorrow. Time for me to be moving along."

The group quickly broke up and paid their checks. A few distributors made a mental note *not* to invite that "do-gooder" distributor to next week's coffee session.

Some people just don't understand why they get paid. They look for the free ride.

"Success is not the result of making the rules easier, but the result of overcoming obstacles!"

~ Tom "Big Al" Schreiter

Tom Schreiter is the author of the *Big Al* books and audiotapes. The article above is an excerpt from his book *Big Al's Turbo MLM* and is reprinted here with the publisher's permission. Tom also publishes the monthly *Fortune Now* newsletter. He and Jan are *Upline®* Masters and were speakers for Networkmarketingtimes.com MLM Millennium Symposium in Los Angeles in 2000.

bigalnews@tntmag.com and www.fortunenow.com
1-281-280-9800
KAAS Publishing:
PO Box 890084, Houston, TX 77289

"Example is not the main thing in influencing others. It is the only thing."
~ Albert Schweitzer

❧ GAVIN SCOTT ❧

I Stuck It Out and Learned A Lot

I HAVE BEEN A DISTRIBUTOR FOR A WONDERFUL COMPANY called Kleeneze in London for the last 7 years. I have listened and watched people come and go, and watched a few stay, lead and prosper. Our company has been retailing home care and fitness products since 1923 and was the first company in Europe to change to a Network Marketing plan in 1970. A lot of people said it would not work any more because it had been around too long, and lots of people had tried it, and quit. However, I chose to build my organization seriously, and today I have over 4,000 distributors.

I worked in the shipyards in London from the age of 16 to 30. I was sick and tired of that kind of work and knew there had to be a better way. I was open to listening to a presentation about Network Marketing. When I was shown a Network Marketing opportunity, I had 6 weeks of sleepless nights with the excitement of the opportunity ahead. I joined Kleeneze in 1992. I have learned a lot from people and have watched my organization ignite from reading *Fire Up!*, Jan Ruhe's book. We have even started carrying it in our company.

I have never been more excited about the future of Network Marketing than I am today. Become a *True Leader*—my best tip is to get yourself into a personal growth and development program. Become a reader, after all readers are leaders and leaders are readers. Here's what else I've learned:

True Leaders:

+ always **leave people feeling better** and more positive after they have spoken with the *True Leader.*

+ have to **build up expert people skills**—the skill to work with top leaders, right down to new people who have just joined the organization.

+ have to **have solid belief,** no matter how hard people try to knock them or their company down.

+ **know** that if people have been successful in their company before, then it's doable for others as well.

True Leaders:

+ **look** for people on their team to develop as leaders themselves. The faster they become leaders and the faster they develop leaders, the faster their business will grow.

+ **never stop learning.** Every day for the past 7 years in Kleeneze, I have worked on learning something new which will help me and my team members.

+ **show 110% belief** in themselves, their company, their products and in the Network Marketing industry.

Gavin Scott's team sold the equivalent of almost $30 million in Kleeneze products during 1999; and his team was paid nearly $15 million in bonuses as a result. His organization now numbers over 4,000. His Kleeneze income exceeds $2 million so far, with $500,000 earned last year alone. Gavin is a friend of Jan's. He lives in England with his girlfriend, Bonnie, and her son.

gavin.scott@virgin.net
international phone number: 00441912595765

Rick Seymour

Leader of Leaders

To build a large organization in MLM one needs to become a *leader of leaders* not a *leader of followers*. I've watched many successful people over the years and have tried to understand how this happens. Here are some of the conclusions I've drawn.

We need to accept people where they are, and *encourage them to become more than they are*. This means personal growth, change and the development of new skills. People tend to resist change. How do we as leaders overcome that resistance?

First and most obviously leaders need a *strong vision for the future*, and more than that, they must be able to *paint others into that vision*. People resist change unless they have a good *reason* to change. Helping them develop a powerful vision and goals gives them the motivation to change and grow and learn.

We need to be willing to ask the tough questions in a way that opens people up to possibilities (I like to call it the 'velvet hammer'). Questions like: "Is your activity sufficient to achieve your goals?" "Are you operating on the right principles?" "Do you need to change?" "If you keep doing what you're doing, will you achieve your goals?"

We must not only know what *we're* doing, but we must be able to *teach someone else* and convince them that we can teach them. Many have the desire, but not the *belief in themselves*. If they believe in your ability to teach them, they will join you.

We all have seen very charismatic leaders that motivate others to excel, but once the leader relaxes or leaves, the organization dies. Charisma is not trainable or duplicable—but a *process is*. It's not enough to inspire—*we must have a process that we can teach to others; a basic set of skills that will give people more competence*. With competence comes confidence and more willingness to take risks and try something new.

To teach and coach others effectively, here are the four parts of the adult learning model:

1. **Model** the desired behavior for them.

2. **Explain the thinking** and rationale behind the behavior, so that if a scenario doesn't unfold exactly as modeled, they will have some idea of how to respond effectively.

3. **Role-play the behavior** with them, so they can begin to visualize the expected outcomes and practice their skills.

4. **Coach them, support them and affirm them** as they begin to practice their new behavior in a safe environment. Continue to recognize them for their successes. Having done all that, make sure you invest your time in those people that have *desire* as well as need. You can't want it worse for them than they want it for themselves. You can't drag someone over the finish line. Do they have the commitment and self-discipline to see their business as a priority? Or does their business get only the time that is left over? (And there's never any left over!)

> "When we invest our time in the right people, doing the right things, we can expect a terrific future!"
>
> ~ Rick Seymour

Rick Seymour was an aerospace engineer for 18 years. He and his wife, Aldona, are Master Coordinators with the Shaklee Corporation and have been in the business part-time for 25 years. They have earned a six-figure income for the last 16 years, and 12 bonus cars. They have been in the company's Presidents Club 14 years, and have been on 35 international award trips. Rick and Aldona Seymour live in Colorado.

1-303-733-9797

> "There are no mistakes so great as that of being always right."
>
> ~ Samuel Butler

ᘓᕠᕐ TODD SMITH ᕽᕽᕿᕝ

The Internet Is The Future

‌⟋⟍

THE NEXT WAVE OF THE FUTURE IS TO BECOME SAVVY and dive headfirst into building your Network Marketing business *online*—not only promoting your Network Marketing business, but promoting *yourself* as well.

Have you heard it said that you should focus on your strengths, and that your weaknesses are irrelevant? Well, I disagree. If there are areas where you are weak, you need to ask yourself if these are areas that are important in becoming a better leader, and if they are, you need to begin to work on improving yourself in those areas.

One of the most important things to work on if you want to be a successful and *True Leader* is to continue to grow as a person. If you are not continuing to strive to be a better person, how can you honestly expect your people to do what you're not doing? Network Marketing is a business of leadership. What you do is what your people will do. The way you lead your organization is how your people will lead their organization. If *you* strive to be the best leader you can be, and strive to help your people become the best leaders *they* can be, then you will enjoy greater success and happiness in your life and in your career. My great success key is focusing on being the best leader I can be and in duplicating that in my people. Being a *True Leader* takes time, energy and effort, and it's a journey not a destination, so never stop striving to be the best.

Things are constantly changing, and one must look into the future and identify new and exciting opportunities. Visionary leaders are constantly looking for ways to improve. The technology revolution is the most significant revolution of our lifetime. It will completely revolutionize industries and change how every business is run. Along with this comes great opportunity for those that look for it. Our industry is in for great change and improvement.

The Internet will provide many new opportunities for Network Marketers: generating leads will be easier than ever before and geographic boundaries will expand. More people will succeed because many of the skills that are required for success today will be irrelevant in the online future. The cost for people to participate will be dramatically reduced—no more sales aids, no more voice mail bills, no inventory, reduced phone bills—the list goes on. People will be so much more effective when they can set up their own .com business that can generate revenue 24 hours a day 7 days a week.

People will no longer have to get outside of their comfort zone to prospect, because they now can begin building relationships online and begin communicating with people online and not be scared when they start prospecting. Inviting people will be easier than ever when all you have to do is send a friend an e-mail with a link to your own personal web site that your company has set up for you. The Network Marketing industry will look completely different in two to three years.

The visionary *True Leaders* that look for opportunity on the Internet and learn how to market themselves and their businesses will be the new leaders of the future. Leadership in Network Marketing is going to be different than in the past.

Get busy figuring out how to get on the Internet. It's the next wave of *True Leadership*. *True Leaders* are already headed that way.

Todd Smith built NuSkin's fastest growing U.S. business after joining in 1990. He broke their growth and income records with his first check of $31,600. In 1991, he joined Rexall Showcase. Todd has earned more than $12 Million in career earnings with Rexall. He is now chairman of the company's presidential Board of Advisors. He and his wife, Joy, live in Florida with their four children. Todd travels the world and shared with Jan that what is really missing worldwide is *True Leadership*.

www.toddsmith.net

"Resolve that whatever you do you will bring the whole man to it, that you will fling the whole weight of your being into it."

~ Orison S. Marden

❦ DAVID STEWART ❦

The Vital Importance
of Field Leaders

$$\sim$$

A *TRUE LEADER* IS ONE WHO INSPIRES AND EMPOWERS individuals to give and be their best in alignment with a common vision. Nowhere is this more important than in the building of a successful Network Marketing organization.

The success of any Network Marketing company ultimately depends on the ability of the most enthusiastic distributors to achieve their individual financial goals through that company. The company may have a great product line, an outstanding income opportunity, powerful sales aids and practical support, yet fail from the lack of consistently strong enthusiasm among its distributors.

The key to such enthusiasm is the constant training and encouragement of those individual distributors. However, that kind of support cannot be provided solely by the company. To be effective, it must also and primarily come from strong field leaders. These *True Leaders* are the essential link between the company and their distributors.

Every distributor needs personal motivation and practical training. It is through the individual guidance of field leaders that a new distributor can best learn organization-building techniques that are congruent with the corporate vision. It is by mastering those techniques and maintaining their personal enthusiasm that a distributor can best realize his or her financial goals.

People willingly follow leaders who speak convincingly from successful experience and who take the same kind of actions that they encourage others to take. A field leader's own successful organization is the example that distributors most willingly follow. It also inspires others to become leaders. *True Leaders* become leaders by building other leaders.

The same is true of companies. By encouraging, supporting, training and motivating productive field leaders, a Network Marketing company can ensure that their leaders are equipped and inspired to do the same for their personal organizations.

With thirty years in Network Marketing, I have yet to see a leading company that does not empower their field leaders to the best of their ability. It is an intricate part of their corporate culture and vision. Conversely, those companies who do not understand or have the capacity to deliver this kind of support, never realize their potential.

The success of any Network Marketing company is directly proportional to their support and the success of its field leadership.

David Stewart has over 30 years of experience in Network Marketing. He has grown an organization to over 100,000 distributors. David founded Success In Action, Inc., an international consulting firm for the Network Marketing industry. David lives in Arizona.

dstewart96@email.msn.com
1-800-488-8505
Success In Action, Inc., Scottsdale, AZ

❧ ALLEN STRUNK ❧

Leadership = Four Key Concepts

⌁

AS I LOOK BACK AT MY LIFE, I HAVE TO SMILE. I FIND IT
so amusing how my perception of what is true and real have
changed. For instance, there is no Santa Claus, there is life
after the Army, and rock and roll did not die. Which brings
me to my perception of something that has really affected and
changed me both personally and professionally—*True
Leadership.*

From my seven-year stint in the U.S. Army to my current
Network Marketing business, I have changed my view and
approach to leadership. In the Army as a Sergeant, I was
afforded the opportunity to attend military leadership training. At these classes, we were taught that leadership was the
ability to get others to react without you physically having to
force them to. Several tactics were taught to us on how to
accomplish this feat. One tactic was to ensure that our soldiers
understood if they did not react without physical motivation,
they would be thrown out of the military. This was accept-
able, for that particular environment, however, we all know
that in the "real" world, a tactic such as this would not stand
a chance.

After my "Army days," and since my involvement with
Network Marketing, I have come to the conclusion that there
are four key leadership concepts: **(1) being Courageous, (2)**

being Observant, (3) Inspiring others, and (4) knowing how to be an excellent Follower.

True Leaders:

+ **assist** you in reaching deep into yourself to find your answers on why and how to continue striving forward.

+ **don't** use threat tactics to force you forward.

+ **improve** themselves both professionally and personally.

+ **inspire** you to continue through your hardships.

+ **know** that recognition is a must to empower their organization.

+ **set** the example and give you a beacon to guide you down your path to success.

True Leaders have:

+ **answers** on why and how to continue striving forward.

+ the **courage** to admit when they are wrong.

True Leaders are:

+ **excellent** followers.

+ in **tune** with the success of each member of their organization and are quick to announce this success in front of their peers.

+ **never** threatened about the possibility of their followers surpassing them, in fact they empower their followers to do so.

+ **never** too proud to ask others for leadership and guidance.

+ **observant** of their follower's progress.

+ **open** to new suggestions on how they can improve, both professionally and personally.

+ **quick** to assist those who are having trouble, if they don't have the answer, they help followers seek out the information that they need.

- **ready** to switch from the role of teacher to student.
- **seek** out new knowledge and tactics to empower both their organization and themselves.

Just as we must choose our own destiny, so must we also choose our own leadership style. Your definition of leadership will be directly related to the values that you decide to emulate. Sometimes the path you choose may affect others, directly or indirectly. Find out what your definition of leadership is, and continue to push yourself to improve!

Allen and Baerbel Strunk are Network Marketers involved in an American Communications Network, CAN. Allen is 29 years old. He and Baerbel live in Germany with their two children.

astrunk@comtrass.com
www.imgnetwork.de
Phone: +49-6003-3755/930015

"Keep true, never be ashamed of doing right; decide on what you think is right and stick to it."

~ George Eliot

ᕼᑎᏗ HASSELINE E. THOMPSON ᕤᏗᏗ

Leadership as Practiced by Southern Women

＿＿＿～＿＿＿

Some enterprising women in Birmingham, Alabama, are presently successfully merchandising a product line called G. R. I. T. S., an acronym for "Girls Raised In The South." Tee shirts, baseball caps, and coffee cups abound with such sentiments as "G. R. I. T. S. know their primary colors: Crimson and White," a reference to the Alabama Crimson Tide football team. Needless to say, these items are best sellers among a measurable segment of the young female market in Alabama. One wonders if the creative producers of G. R. I. T. S. have considered expanding beyond school loyalties, possibly producing products that proclaim other pithy thoughts such as "G. R. I. T. S. know their place—*any place they want to be.*" Or would that message be dead on arrival in the heart of Dixie?

Growing up female in the South is a unique experience. In books and movies the "southern belle" has been lauded more for her beauty and charm than for her intelligence and accomplishments. Even today Southern women find themselves struggling with the burden of presenting the expected feminine image, highly prized and rewarded in the South, while actively pursuing their goals and aspirations. So, under these circumstances, how do the women of this world emerge and prosper?

A certain amount of fearlessness is mandatory to female success in the South, as this is a culture that loves for women to compromise and encourages men to maintain the status quo. *True Leadership* necessitates the ability to make one's case with conviction and, occasionally, even passion. Not giving in to the urge to please at all costs, choosing delicacy under duress at the expense of results, requires a particular brand of bravery from the Southern woman. The one who takes her position with true presence will soon gather disciples and move on with her program. It takes courage, however, to step out of the crowd, and only a *True Leader is willing to risk her standing and reputation in pursuit of the greater goal.*

Being competitive, often in the name of a higher standard, is frequently the hallmark of a young leader. A telling example is the Greek sorority system as it functions in the South. While there are many reasons, social among them, why sororities flourish in this region, the system is strong also because these organizations support competitive behavior in the pursuit of excellence. Loyalty to the "house" and its standards energizes these young women who perform major feats, individually and collectively, in philanthropy, campus-wide competitions and elections, and honorary organizations. Setting competitive goals and deadlines becomes a way of life where finishing second best is unacceptable. Competing to be the best is part and parcel of the Greek leader who believes that competition for a good purpose always matters.

One of the finest tools of *True Leadership* is the Southern woman's ability to diplomatically weave her way to her goal when confronted with potential opposing forces. In a culture dedicated to civility above most everything else, political astuteness is a requirement of success and is especially effective when it is tempered with the characteristic sincere charm of the Southern lady. Practicing the art of diplomacy is, without a doubt, a major trump card in the Southern female arsenal, where all can be achieved without the sacrifice of one's principles.

Girls raised in the South do in fact know their place, and *it is any place they want to be.* They have, in fact, been leading for years in their own canny way. Conviction of purpose, achievement through honest competition, and political savvy are not strange rituals to these committed women. After all, as G.R.I.T.S. know, being "number one" has been a sacred Southern tradition for a long time.

Hasseline E. Thompson is the Rush and Pledge Advisor for the Phi Mu Sorority at The University of Alabama. She and her husband, Art Thompson, live in Alabama and Aspen, Colorado. She has been president of numerous civic and professional boards and was one of the top real estate agents in Tuscaloosa, Alabama for years. Hasseline is a close personal friend of Jan's. Art and Jan were with Hasseline and her daughter, Polly Beth, on the 1999 Network Marketing Millennium Leadership Cruise.

athompson@cba.ua.edu
1-205-349-2110

༺ DRACY WOODS ༻

Be A Leader

To SHARE WISDOM YOU MUST FIRST HAVE EXPERIENCE, and to have experience, you must have the willingness to try. If you develop willingness, a positive attitude and good work ethic you can become a *True Leader*. It's all about becoming someone bigger and greater than you are today. As a great start on your journey of leadership challenges, "Fake it till you make it." Here are several quotes that I love and don't know who to give the credit to:

> **"Only those willing to fail greatly, will ever succeed greatly."**
>
> **"Have a backbone, not just a wishbone."**
>
> **"Speed not perfection."**
> **~ PartyLite's Philosophy**

With a backbone comes the discipline to develop your weaknesses into your strengths. This will help you become a *True Leader*.

Get excited about the journey of *True Leadership*! Know your *why*! Why do you want to become great? What lights that fire in your heart that makes you greet the dawn with enthusiasm? Knowing this allows you to bloom through adversity. The *True Leaders* have depth of vision.

What do you see for yourself and those around you? What do you see when you look at an acorn? What do you see when you look at your starter kit? Free product? Cash? A hot tub, vacations, new wardrobe, a six-digit income? *What I see is an opportunity to release the shackles of poverty, not just for yourself, but for generations after you! Imagine!*

To realize your vision, get an idea of *how* you are going to get there. Get a direction that is moving forward, study the compensation plan, and learn what it takes to get to the top of your company. Look at the top position as a gold medal from the Olympics. Achieve it, then you can coach others to do the same!

Build great relationships, become influential through your character and honesty. Have a raw enthusiasm! People will follow you because it is contagious. Your integrity and a genuine compassion for your team will have an everlasting result.

Surround yourself with people who want *for* you, not *from* you. Your environment is so important. Share your dreams only with positive people. Spend *minutes* with negative people and *hours* with people who are going in the same direction as you. Take advice from those that have what you want—health, happiness, prosperity, spiritual fulfillment, and relationships.

Turn hope into *action*, and show others how to do the same. Consistently encourage others, believe in them and their future, give them the tools! And give them the know-how to build confidence so *they too* can grow and excel and develop into something so miraculous.

> ## "We are all like fine pieces of silver, no matter how young or how old, we always need polishing."
> ### ~ Dracy Woods

My life philosophy is everything I do, I do it for the children. If every decision I make, every step I take, every word I utter is guided by the thought that a child is observing me, I will always do the right thing. I am grateful.

The quote that has always kept me from having the arrival syndrome is:

> ## "A master is not judged by how many followers they have but by how many masters they've created."
> ### ~ Jim Rohn

Dracy Woods was a single mom on welfare with a two-year-old and a foster child at the age of 15. She started in party plan at age 24 and in her first full year of business made a six-digit income. It took her four months to become a leader, then within 12 more months, Dracy and her team promoted 12 leaders. She attended her first national conference as a consultant, and the next year was a Senior Regional VP for PartyLite Gifts, Canada. She now makes multi-six digits and is striving to make an annual seven-digit income. She lives on Vancouver Island with her husband and four children.

adwoods@pacificcoast.net

❧ RENE REID YARNELL ❧

The Seeds of Leadership are Born out of Adversity

BEHIND ALL THE FAÇADE, BENEATH THE EXTERNALS, what is it to be a leader? I mean, a *True Leader*. When I think of leaders I strive to emulate and mentally amalgamate all of their qualities into action steps, certain characteristics emerge and, surprisingly, in an orderly progression. The more selfless the leader, the more integrity pervades the outcome. But from where does leadership germinate? How does it evolve into moving others to action? The seeds of leadership are born out of adversity.

True Leaders are:

- ♦ **cause-oriented.**
- ♦ **fearless** in their pursuits.
- ♦ the **teacher** and the **student** coupled into a single ongoing process. It is a revolving, ever-maturing process of listening, learning, and leading; listening, learning, and leading.
- ♦ **uncaring** about what others might think of their actions.

True Leaders:

- ♦ **assuage** people's self-doubts and insecurities in the process of taking them from one paradigm to another, from a familiar place to a more risky one.
- ♦ **believe,** beyond any doubt, in their own power to effect change. It is not a question of *if* but *when* it will happen.

- **bring** about worthwhile changes that result in bringing the human and sacred world they touch closer in alignment to oneness, to goodness, to love.

- **build** on their own strengths and strive to complement their weaknesses with the strengths of others.

- **create** an environment that brings out the best in others, passing on to them the will to carry out a common goal.

- **develop** a balance in their lives and their perspectives.

- **develop** an ability to create one unified body out of many diverse members, making the whole greater than the sum of its parts.

- **do not overreact** to either praise or blame.

- **effect change.** The more *visionary* the leader, the more *dynamic* the impact of such change.

- **empower** others to do what they did not know they could do, encouraging them to rise to their fullest potential.

- **emerge** from many crises, admittedly bruised and scarred. And as victors, they begin to feel the power of their own inner-strength. They not only know that they pulled themselves out of the depths of a seemingly insurmountable situation, but they also gradually develop a security and confidence in *knowing* that if they did it once, *they can do it again.* Such self-belief begins to radiate, like an aura, in the form of positive energy touching all those who come within their range. It has a magnetic quality that draws others in and, perhaps unconsciously, makes them want to share in its ecstasy.

- **err** on the side of understatement rather than on the side of exaggeration.

- **have** faced the greatest challenges and *overcome them* again and again.

- **help** others discover and commit to their own convictions.

- ♦ **know** how to deal with their own challenges before they can guide others to do the same.
- ♦ know that leadership is not about coercion.
- ♦ **listen.** And through listening they are *learning.* The Japanese word for teacher is *sensei,* which means honored leader.
- ♦ **must first** be able to *lead themselves* before they can lead others.
- ♦ **organize** their own vision and purpose in such a way that they will inspire their followers toward the same end.
- ♦ **see** life as a mission, an uncharted sea to be discovered, a less traveled road to walk down.
- ♦ **strive** to smooth out the jagged edges of their overachievement and to enhance those areas of their lives that are not nearly developed enough.
- ♦ **understand** people's fear of change.

Rene Reid Yarnell is a former Catholic nun, who became an elected politician and businesswoman. Today she teaches, writes, and consults for the Network Marketing industry. With her partner, she created a 200,000-person organization, moving $70 million in products through 27 countries. She is co-author of the national bestseller *Your First Year in Network Marketing* and author of *The New Entrepreneurs.* She and Jan are interviewed on *The Woman's Tapes.* Rene is a friend of Jan's.

rene@yarnell.com
www.yarnell.com

Chapter 2

How to Build True Leaders by Mastering People

—✎—

Art Burleigh and Jan Ruhe

IF YOU WANT TO BUILD *TRUE LEADERS,* YOU MUST BE ABLE to master people and not ask them to do anything you aren't willing to do yourself. You can be the *True Leader* in all the business, social, political and neighborhood activities in which you choose to participate. Want to learn a technique that will motivate unmotivated people, professional people, your spouse and children? This chapter will teach you just how to do that.

Many people try to *convert* others into permanent *True Leaders* for their business—whether they are doctors, lawyers, ministers, politicians, parents, Network Marketers or other professionals. However, from our experience we know that Network Marketers need to *build True Leaders* and help make *them* successful.

Whether you have a large or small Network, built with only a few people in your successline, *spend your main efforts on building True Leaders.*

It may be that at this time in your life, you might not be in the position to concern yourself with building leaders, but when that day comes, as we're sure it will, the information in this chapter will be of tremendous value to you.

Do you ever wonder why some companies are unable to retain their highly skilled people? Why do some companies have constant turnover of their trained personnel? Here's the answer: *They do not fulfill the basic needs and desires of their people.*

How is it that highly *successful* companies *are* able to retain the loyal services of their sales people for a lifetime? Once again, the answer is simple: *They fulfill the needs and desires of their people.*

So, if you want to build a network with *True Leaders*, do exactly what these top companies do: *fulfill people's needs and desires so they will become your loyal followers.*

If you want your spouse to be loyal and faithful to you, make sure you take care of his or her needs and desires. Then you'll never end up in divorce court wondering what happened.

Here are some great benefits you will get when you build *True Leaders*.

People will:
- **feel** *they belong*, a human need.
- **respect** you, trust you and have full confidence in you.
- **stick by you** when the going gets rough. And believe us, the going gets rough for *True Leaders* on occasion.
- willingly **give** you their loyal cooperation and whole-hearted support.
- **work** hard to show you that they can get the job done.
- **work** *together as a team* with high spirit and morale, with passion, conviction, purpose and dedication toward a common goal. Group growth and momentum will develop. Powerful duplication will occur!

Loyalty begins with you. If you want people to be loyal to you and follow you, *give them your loyalty first*. If you are the

Upline, you must set the example for your people to follow by being loyal to your own Upline. No matter what, we never cut down our Uplines, never. Jan's Upline in her company made a very difficult choice and took her own life in the late 1980s. Jan, to this day, thanks her Upline for helping her get started.

Here is how to develop this quality of loyalty from your successline:

1. Be quick to **defend** your successline and Upline from abuse.

2. **Never** give the slightest hint of disagreement with your Upline's philosophy when relaying his/her success principles to your own successline. If you do disagree with your Upline's philosophy, tell the Upline, never dump down.

3. Do every part of your business to the best of your ability. **Go for greatness.** This shows your loyal support of your Upline's wishes.

4. **Never discuss the personal challenges** of your successline with others. If a person tells you something that is confidential, respect that confidence.

5. **Stand up** for your people when they are unjustly accused. Nothing is worse than being falsely accused. Shame on those who build their businesses bad-mouthing their Upline. They certainly are not *True Leaders.* Remember the Golden Rule.

6. **Never criticize your Upline** in front of your successline. You cannot expect loyalty from below if you are not loyal to those above. There are no statues erected to the critics anyway, anywhere.

Instead of concentrating on "getting" something out of your company, use your creativity to move more products and *then* you will make more money for yourself. If your company is treating you fairly, has a great product, delivers products on time, pays your check on time, recognizes *fairly all achievements,* does not play favorites and handles customer service well—then the company never has to worry about not having **loyal distributors.** A distributor's loyalty to a company stems from the company's loyalty to its distributors. Pay the most attention to your top distributors in your organization. The needs and desires of all distributors are: **financial security, need for recognition** and **status, a feeling of pride in one's work, accomplishments** and **fairness.** If you are having trouble with your distributors then we suggest that you go over and over this list until you *meet the needs of all your distributors.* (Warning: don't play favorites.) It's not about meeting your own needs.

A training system has been another one of our keys to success to promote *True Leaders.* We have discovered that when you train people as a team, you give them, each one of them, a sense of being needed and wanted and the feeling of belonging. One of the strongest psychological drives in a person is the *desire to belong* and have identification with a group. When distributors know that they are wanted, that their work is appreciated, and that their efforts are contributing to the achievement of a worthwhile team goal, then the pride kicks in and they will be proud of their own work and proud of the team.

This brings out the *True Leaders.*

When you promote a strong sense of *team*, they will have a feeling of pride and loyalty. Your job will be so much fun and easier when you embrace the ideas of your budding leaders. When the chips are down, *True Leaders* respond and support the Upline as members of a well-trained and loyal sales organization.

Teamwork starts at the top *and* bottom. It goes both directions simultaneously. To be really effective, it must spread laterally as well. The smart, effective leaders get their successline to work together as one big team for the common good, and then all can gain maximum results. Those whose mission is to "train the field" are not *True Leaders* in our industry. Period.

Establish an emotional rallying point for people in your successline to gather around. As examples, consider these exciting ideas:

- ◆ "Let's knock the company's socks off this month with each of us selling $500 in product!"
- ◆ "Let's go for promoting 10 *True Leaders!*"
- ◆ "Let's go for broke this month, pull out all the stops and sponsor 50 new people together!"
- ◆ "Let's make a difference in the lives of others, because as we know, our products make a difference!"

Intangible goals are impossible for the average person to visualize, for they are too abstract and vague. They do not inspire or stir a person into massive action, or to become a *True Leader*. It's not easy to establish an emotional rallying point so you can be a *True Leader*. However, if you put your creativity, initiative and ingenuity to work, it can be done. **Believe us, the results are worth it!**

True Leaders understand how important spouse support is in building and maintaining a sales organization. The very best method to use to insure your spouse's loyalty is to go out of your way to fulfill every single one of their basic needs and desires. A lot of couples help out at home, and spend their entire day in the home, taking care of the children, the bills and they get no appreciation or recognition whatever from their spouse for what they do. If you neglect your spouse's needs and desires and take him or her for granted, you might find yourself in divorce court. In this day and time, 50% of all marriages end in divorce. You can't give your spouse too much appreciation. And, by the way, it goes both ways.

You don't have to send flowers or candy on a daily basis to show how much someone is worth or appreciated. Here's what we suggest: pay special, close attention to your spouse. Always let your spouse know that you are aware they are around and that you appreciate them. Remember the magic words, *please* and *thank you*. When you pass each other in the house, just reach out and touch your spouse gently. Little things. It's been our desire to have a loving spouse with a harmonious relationship, and we want our spouses to be loyal to us. If you want that as well, then give your wholehearted attention to your spouse. *True Leadership* is not just about business, it's about how you live your life.

Okay, you have to listen to others, we all agree on that. But then what? Here's what we have found that works. Keep people talking to learn more about what's important to the prospect. *True Leaders* know to use these four magic phrases:

1. "And then, what did you do?"
2. "And then, what did you say?"
3. "Please tell me about it."
4. "Can you say more about that?"

It's quite easy to manage people. It's quite easy to take the perfect combination of good and well-trained people to build a team. That's really no challenge at all. Anyone can do that.

True Leaders know that they are measured by what gets done, the bottom line. It's only the results that count, not the effort. Even if you feel that you may be a common, ordinary person, you can become a *True Leader* by just spending a few minutes a day improving yourself. You will become vastly more powerful than you ever dreamed possible before. If all the people in this book could do it, then so can you. So, go on, make yourself into the *True Leader* you are meant to be. We are cheering you on!

Chapter 3

Creating Team Spirit

Art Burleigh and Jan Ruhe

Have you ever played on a winning athletic team? Have you ever been part of a group that achieved an unusual record of results in business, sports or anywhere else? Both Art's son Seth and Jan's daughter Ashley were high school soccer stars. Jan's son Clayton broke three Colorado state football records in high school! We have been around high school sports for years, and it is very exciting.

There is often a special thrill to sports. We watched the feelings that our children got from working together with their teams to accomplish something that no *one* of them could have achieved alone. Yes, maybe there were a few stars that were more important than others, in their own way. Yet *everyone* contributed to the team; everybody had a part to play; everybody got credit. Everybody had a good reason to feel proud and satisfied with what he or she contributed and what the *whole team* accomplished.

If you are a leader, *that's* the spirit you are trying to create, the feeling among your associates, your team members, *that they are an important part of a winning team*. That's what an outstanding company president, coach or an Upline strives to do—so does a good division leader, department chief, supervisor, manager or foreman. It does not matter what level you work at; the principles are the same. If you want the best possible results, you must give people the feeling that they are part of a winning team, and that each one of them is an *important* part.

How do you build this kind of spirit? It all lies in *your attitude*. The only thing you really have control over is your attitude. Attitudes are contagious . . . is *yours* worth catching? How do you feel about the people in your successline or those you supervise? Do you think of them as working *for* you or *with* you? If your basic attitude reflects the idea that people are working *for* you, that you are the key person and they are like dominoes you push around, you will *never* bring any group to its full potential.

Building great team spirit starts with knowing your team and the talents of each player—and *then* developing intuition about their individual *potential*. Think back on when *you* may have had a supportive coach . . .

Did that coach:

- ◆ put a lot of **positive emphasis** on what you did well?
- ◆ **believe** in your overall potential?
- ◆ **expect** the very best from you?
- ◆ **take your mistakes in stride** and know that mistakes are human?
- ◆ **help you focus** on *one area at a time* to strengthen rather than overwhelm you with many suggestions for improvements?
- ◆ **keep a positive, winning attitude?**
- ◆ **believe** that a mistake is a failure *only if* you fail to take the opportunity to learn from it?

Have you had a supportive coach in your life? How well did you work for that person? *True Leadership* is about *building leaders* who are successful. When you do this, teamwork will start to develop automatically. No one wants to be taken for granted or feel that they are just tools to be used. Love people and use things—don't use people and love things. Working with a great Upline or empowering management leaders is stimulating. It makes people feel that they really belong, that they are important parts of a *team*!

Be sure to communicate. Keep your leaders informed—it's vital to developing team spirit. Nobody likes to be on the outside. Make decisions *after consulting* with your people. They will feel more important and will be more interested in the team's pursuit of exciting goals.

Talk to people who are in your organization, let them know what you are thinking. Let them know what you are planning. Talk *with* them as if it were *their* organization, *their* business, as well as yours—because it absolutely is! Understand their ideas and suggestions, and evaluate their validity. Ask questions, get your team members to think—*and dream!* Help them to see and embrace ideas for success that used to be out of their reach—or even unimaginable. Share the success and credit that comes your way.

Team Spirit Building Qualities of the *True Leader*:

- ◆ **take risks.**
- ◆ **stay focused.**
- ◆ **be persistent.**
- ◆ **be courageous.**
- ◆ **have a thick skin.**
- ◆ **have a charging spirit.**
- ◆ **stay alert—for both danger *and* opportunity.**

A great Upline is not someone who has been raised to a level above others and sits on a throne. They share the job and the challenges with all the leaders in the group and coordinate their efforts.

In football, all great ball carriers give tremendous credit to the linemen and backs who run interference for them. They are quick to share credit and praise. Why? *Because it's the right thing to do.* It is the right thing to do as a *True Leader* too. You can't have an explosive business without an attitude and behavior pattern that creates and supports Team Spirit!

The pursuit of success can sometimes be lonely. It's a lot more fun with excited teammates who eagerly support you on the journey *and celebrate with you* at each milestone. Become great at building Team Spirit!

Are You Waiting?

For someone to lead and inspire you?

For the boss to recognize you?

For clients to thank you?

For coworkers to help you?

For the world to hail you?

For your Upline or boss to recognize
your achievements?

For your home office to appreciate and value you?

Well, here's a news flash . . .

They are all just sitting there, too.

Waiting for you!

Chapter 4

True Leaders Are Guides
Around Land Mines

―――

Art Burleigh and Jan Ruhe
With Contributions from Randy Gage

T*RUE LEADERS* ARE JUST LIKE GUIDES. KEEP FOCUSED ON that. When you are a *True Leader* you are like a guide. *You are a guide.* Whether you are a tour guide, a sporting guide, a travel guide, a guide to information, or any other kind of a guide, you are a *leader*. People look to guides to help them and guide them safely to where they are going, to have a wonderful and pleasant journey to the information. What if you started out on an adventure and it turned into a nightmare and you stepped on a land mine? Someone could have guided you and told you not to enter that particular area. However, without the guide, you plowed on ahead and now are paying the price, forever.

As we were writing this book, we had many conversations about our experiences and found that building leaders and *making them successful* was not easy and that we had found some very destructive land mines through the years which those of you in Network Marketing will absolutely want to avoid! Be careful as you go through building a business. There are probably many more land mines we could have chosen to include here; this is a place for you to start. Pay attention, this is important information. Share it with your upcoming leaders—you will be so glad you did!

You are so very *important*. Your role as a guide is often critical to the success of others. And when you help others succeed, you succeed! Success breeds success.

When you begin your path to *True Leadership* in Network Marketing, you know that you must begin to sponsor others into your business so that you can have a pool of people to begin to work with to promote leaders.

When your new distributors start into partnership with you in your organization, they have a short time period of about 90-120 days to get their business started before they reach "the crossroads with you and your venture." At this point, they are either on track towards the "highway of success" or they are headed right back to their old situation— their old job track.

As *True Leaders*, it is our responsibility to help these people make the correct decision—for them. Either to progress into higher, more committed partnership with us on the highway to success or, to either explore other options or return to where they seem destined to stay—in their old rut, in their jobs they often "hate." For some people, that second choice is the *right* decision—for *them*. Some people just can't muster the internal drive and self-motivation to elevate themselves into the stimulating arena of success—they are too afraid of the commitment and effort it takes to propel themselves to a whole new level of lifestyle and achievement. Sad, but too true—don't prolong their agony!

So how and where do you start the process of being a *True Leader?* The process starts with learning how to manage *yourself*—before you think you can possibly "manage" or lead others. It's far better to teach others how to manage or lead *themselves*. We are *independent* contractors, *not* dependent contractors.

Helping others succeed often depends on self-awareness, experience and knowledge of what we call Network Marketing land mines that *True Leaders* have learned to avoid.

True Leaders identify and avoid land mines, and they help their organization avoid them, especially the new people who are headed towards the crossroads! Dangerous land mines can certainly cause frustration and discouragement, if not serious destruction of your business! Whenever you get frustrated in the future, you can usually check back to this list and see which land mines have been stepped on, either by your new distributors, *or even by you!*

Ready? Are you really ready to help yourself become a *True Leader?* Here come the land mines to avoid! Get your highlighter out and pay close attention! Navigate around all of these, and watch your bank account grow and grow! Come on, get really excited, this is the first time this information has gone into print. Oh, how we wish we had had this information early on in our careers. Onward to expose and explore land mines!

Here are the 21 key land mines to recognize and avoid on the highway to success.

The Land Mines

1. Stop Retailing—Retailing is the lifeblood of our business. What seems to happen to many Networkers after they start building a little organization is that they tend to become "managers." When we stop retailing our products, we start losing income. We want to "manage" others. **Stop right there.** You cannot quit retailing. Once retailing stops, that "instant money" quits coming in, and it can cause people to start losing their confidence. They begin to doubt the viability of their opportunity, because less income is being generated.

What happens next? The organization doesn't get built as quickly or as strongly as it was starting to when we first began. People buying and using the products create customer satisfaction and more word of mouth enthusiasm for the *benefits* customers appreciate from the products—and it continues to bolster the *belief* of new Network Marketers. And *belief* is critical—every step of the way!

Another benefit that we get from retailing is that it's easier for us there to share the opportunity behind our products. If we quit retailing, what happens is we stop sponsoring—and that kills the growth of our organization.

Summary: The first land mine we tend to step on is that we stop retailing, which slows down prospecting, sponsoring and training.

Result: Our income goes down, our belief system falters, and we stop recruiting and certainly are not viewed as providing *True Leadership*.

Truth: If you want your *organization* to be selling, *you* had better be selling. If you want your organization to be sponsoring, *you* had better be sponsoring. *True Leaders* are always looking for two to three new emerging leaders.

Commit Now! "I will continue retailing and sponsoring, every day, every way! Two new friends a day brings freedom my way!

---

2. **Premature Full Time**—When we quit a job of $30,000–$75,000 per year to jump in full time to our new Network Marketing adventure with our sheer enthusiasm, it's very unrealistic to expect that the former income will be replaced immediately from our new business. Network Marketing income takes some time to develop, be patient. Your organization needs to grow and develop some momentum. *True Leaders* have to be found and trained. That takes time. Bills don't get paid when cash flow to the household drops. We suggest you keep sponsoring and training.

When should you go full time? When you intuitively know that the moment is right for you. When enough replacement income has been flowing steadily, and your company seems stable enough to provide you with a viable, ongoing business vehicle. It could take a couple years to see that things are right to switch to full time; or you could feel that the time to switch occurs much sooner.

When a person quits a full-time job, they are likely to lose contact with the bulk of the warm market prospects, those people with whom they have built relationships. Every day working an 8-5 job, how many people do you come in contact with? A lot. That's usually a very important resource for Network Marketing business builders—a big base of warm market.

Summary: Build your Network Marketing business part time, don't quit your job prematurely. Get some massive results first.

Result: Premature full time can cause financial stress and pressure.

Truth: *True Leaders* are always looking for 2-3 new emerging leaders.

Commit Now! "I will not quit my job until my Network Marketing income gets to a point that it makes sense to go full time with my Network Marketing future!"

---

3. **Unrealistic Expectations**—Many times we hear about what seems like "instant" success by other people within a fairly short time. Often, we tend to think, "if they can do it, so can I." It seems logical until you realize that the pace of someone else's success can be the result of their drive and determination, or it may well be based on *decades* of Network Marketing experience they have had with other companies and or experience *and contacts* they have generated before in dealing with the public. That experience and those contacts can become a huge springboard for the success of others. If you do not have those valuable contacts at first, your expectation of strong income early on is probably very unrealistic.

This can be a very emotional area, especially for the uninformed or idealistic. A large income one month, or a new title you get because you have one or two leaders in your organization, doesn't mean "you have arrived as a *True Leader*" and there will not be income dips as your organization grows and matures. The solution is setting both short-term and long-term goals. When you do, you will know the direction you are headed and you have a plan to get there. *Expect* that roller coaster ride for a while, otherwise, you might lose your courage, passion, enthusiasm and quest to become successful.

Do not promise people the moon. Paint a realistic picture for them so they know that Network Marketing is not a get rich scheme. It takes time, hard work and a program of personal growth and development to achieve *True Leadership*. Plug people into the support tools, systems and the power sources that are working in your organization or company so they can duplicate what truly works.

Summary: Have realistic expectations.

Result: Disappointment abounds if you are unrealistic.

Truth: N.D.A.O.P.C.C. = Never do anything other people can't copy. *True Leaders* are always looking for two to three new emerging leaders.

Commit Now! "I will keep my expectations realistic and will stay fired up, every day, every way!"

---

4. **Not using the Internet to grow and expand your business**—It is not necessary to travel long distances to initially build your Network Marketing business either nationwide or worldwide. With the Internet you can begin an e-mail loop (a regular, recurring e-mail "blast" of helpful news and info to your team); have teleconferencing calls; and create a web page to become connected via technology, instead of spending the money and time at the beginning to actually travel far to train others. As your organization grows, we believe that traveling to meet people on your team is of utmost importance.

Just how important is the Internet for Network Marketing? The Internet has revolutionized the world.

The Internet is bigger than the industrial revolution, the agricultural revolution, the wheel, the light bulb, the automobile, the telephone, the satellite and the television all rolled into one.

The Internet is changing our lives more than all of those things combined, *and faster!* The Internet shrinks our entire world down to an enormous incredible *community.* It allows the consumer to control what he or she gets, and allows them to get it right away. Network Marketing was one of the pioneers on the Internet. Network Marketing led the way!

Serious business builders understand the value of expanding their team into other geographic areas—distant states, provinces or foreign countries, and the Internet is a powerful tool to facilitate this. Developing your skills in using e-mail and the support from business building web sites will accelerate your group's growth. Most Network Marketing companies support their field with company-created web sites that are available to virtually every distributor.

Plus, there are other generic industry web sites that offer powerful business building training and support. These include: fireup.com, SoarToFreedom.com, mlm-metro.com, Upline.com, mlmu.com, and others popping up all the time.

Training new recruits is very important. *Whether it is face-to-face or over the Internet*, whether local or long-distance, training and communicating with your organization is very important. Network Marketing is based upon *building relationships.* Good, caring, supportive and influential *communications* build relationships, and you can *start* building relationships over the phone, teleconferencing and e-mail. Get a digital camera and take photos to beam around the nation or world so that people can see the big picture and appreciate the uniqueness of who you are and the fun of being on your team! Jan put a photo of her glittery "millennium celebration shoes" on fireup.com one month to let everyone around the world see the shoes she was wearing to celebrate the new millennium worldwide! This creates fun—and that's missing too often! A picture is worth what? 1,000 words!

Building relationships can certainly *start* on e-mail and through teleconferencing and personal calls. In the past, many giant Network Marketing organizations started around a kitchen table or in a living room. Then people would have to travel to various locations and meet their expanding organizations. *Today,* you can save travel expenses at first by building your organization over the Internet. Then, you might want to consider traveling and staying in distant cities for a few days on a recurring basis when your long-distance groups begin to grow enough so that a visit by you will clearly provide a significant boost. Make no doubt about it, you will ultimately want to build a long-distance team for stability of your residual income. As you sponsor lots of people in your own hometown, some of those will move to other cities and will start their own organizations there. They too can take advantage of e-mail and teleconferencing and other technology to remain in close communication with you and with their growing team.

Many people want to have someone *else* train their people, or let the company do training. The better way is when *you,* their *True Leader,* actually do the face-to-face or online training yourself. It's a fact that others will not work with people in your organization like *you* would work with them. Even when your corporate office does training online, we have found that in Network Marketing: **the bond is always developed between the new recruit and the person who trains them.** So, make sure that *you* are e-mailing, teleconferencing and helping your new recruits to grow and prosper in your business.

Until you're able to actually visit your long-distance teams in person, consider supporting them by **using all of these communications tools:**

1. **The Telephone**—keep in touch, guide them into staying plugged in to your conference calls and other training calls by both the company (if those calls are made by people who get results and who are ethical) and your Upline (providing that your Upline is walking the talk). The Internet can provide free long-distance phone connections with modest investments of software and equipment.

2. **Speaker Phone**—get your long-distance teams assembled in living rooms or kitchens and use the speaker phone there to train them in a group. You can be home; they can be together at their local Upline's home, and their group synergy will strengthen the impact of your training and mentoring. Keep a regular schedule on these until that local leader can take over.

3. **The Internet**—set up inexpensive video camera hook ups between you in your home office and members of your team—either individually, in their home offices at their computers or even in a larger room where teams are assembled. This Internet technology uses inexpensive software, like CUSeeMe, along with a small video camera, microphone and speakers at each location to facilitate live, interactive visual and voice communications over the Internet for free.

The *True Leader* takes responsibility to train and mentor the people they recruit/sponsor to their fullest potential. The best way to develop an area is by developing the *people* there. If you have more experience in your program than they do, you might wish to begin with a "virtual visit," so they can get off to a good strong start. You can be there *virtually* right away and then travel to those locations as soon as your income allows.

Communicating to keep in touch is so valuable. The group will explode when you go for a visit and fire them way up. Just try it—you will see massive action. Start small, look over the wall, and think tall!

If new distributors lack prior Network Marketing experience, don't worry. Just begin with a duplicable training online, or get Jan Ruhe's Duplicatable Training System (not the only way but a proven way—order online from www.janruhe.com) to help them see, understand and feel the excitement of what is possible for them. Always work on developing two to three leaders in your organization, either locally, nationally or worldwide.

Summary: Begin long distance groups with the Internet, e-mail, teleconferencing, newsletters and personal phone calls. Stay current with communications technology; don't be scared of it.

Result: Your business will boom in areas away from your home base. You can continue to build locally while nationwide or worldwide your business will blossom. Smart use of cutting-edge communications tools can maximize your group's growth potential and that of your income!

Truth: *True Leaders* are always looking for two to three new emerging leaders, and they master the Internet and all the exciting new communications tools.

> **Commit Now!** "I will use the best-available communications tools to strongly build my entire group so it can expand as quickly as possible."

Now, the land mines start getting more serious. *If retailing has stopped, and people have gone prematurely full time into Network Marketing, household income will be down. Frustrations will set in, the marriage is often strained severely, unrealistic expectations set in, maybe there's too much geography to cover, and what suddenly appears is what seems like a real attractive solution to all this.*

It's not! So watch out for . . .

5. **The Quick Fix**—Have you ever noticed anyone in your organization—or maybe *you* have done this—who, when things were going bad, starts talking about some type of Quick Fix? It's amazing that people will quit doing the things that built their early success when they somehow latch onto the idea that those successful strategies can just be ignored in favor of some "Big Deal."

There's nothing wrong with a "Big Deal." A few *can* be landed, so stay alert to opportunity; but those who *set out* to land "Big Deals" will often get sidelined by all the details that can often go wrong. The lesson: Don't *set out* to do "Big Deals." The quickest way to get to know someone is through Networking. Use the wisdom and experience of *people* in your own organization to see what possibilities are there for you. Contacts abound if you are alert for them.

All too often, when a distributor starts "going down," you can listen and watch for them to start looking for a quick way out. They begin to either look for the "Big

Deal," or start talking about the "back burner." Ask yourself if *you* are trying to land a "Big Deal." How much time and energy is that costing you? Could you use that same *huge* amount of time and energy to prospect and sponsor three to five new people this week? Probably! *True Leaders* are always looking for two to three emerging leaders.

"Big Deals" *take a long time to bring to fruition! Calling, talking, flying, working, following up—it goes on and on and on!* The solution? Get back to doing the basics, what got you to where you are, and do not look for the "Big Deals." Get back to plugging into the best support resources, attending meetings and training seminars, sharing the products and opportunity, working your prospect list and on your personal growth and development. When you start looking for "Big Deal" is when the building of the business stops. Watch out for this Leadership land mine! "Big Deals" are a sign of people sliding right down the scale in income and possibly losing money and vision of what is possible through building *relationships*.

And, keep in mind that getting "Big Deals" is not duplicable. In Network Marketing, remember N.D.A.O.P.C.C.; never do anything other people can't copy. Get back to basics! Our job in Network Marketing is to move product, sponsor, train and promote leaders.

Summary: "Big Deals" are not the way to True Leadership in Network Marketing.
Result: The Network does not get built.
Truth: *True Leaders* are always looking for two to three people to develop into leaders.

Commit Now! "I will stick to the basics!"

---

6. **The Answer**—It's when you start hearing people in your group say, "I know what it is . . " or "I know what's wrong" or "We need to change that program, that's what it is . . ." or "I've been looking at this thing, and you know, I just feel like *if* you would just . . ." or "*If* we can call the home office and just change the program" or "I know . . ."

Many companies appreciate your feedback and will consider your suggestions. The reality is if the program needs to be changed, it normally takes a long time and usually the top people have the influence to change the program. Experienced *True Leaders* didn't get to the top of an organization because they were unaware, untalented or inexperienced or had not figured out the Network Marketing concept. Those at the top leading the field are normally the ones to affect changes that are needed. It's up to the *True Leaders* to stick to the basics: *True Leaders* are always looking for two to three people in their organization to move into leadership. Are you getting our drift?

Usually it's the people *not* making any money who always have "The Answer." When they feel themselves getting discouraged and going down, and they begin to play the blame-game, blaming everything else besides themselves for their business downturn. They are usually whining that "The program's wrong." If anyone in your company is making money and if product sales are steady or increasing, the program's probably fine—perhaps it is you who needs a check-up from the neck up! Hmm . . . something to think about.

Another sign of "The Answer" is when you hear people saying "If." As in "You know, Art or Jan, I was watching you in the presentation and *if* . . ." or "*If* you would just . . ." or "*If* we could only . . ." It's always *if*.

True Leaders do not need to yield to the *Ifers*. Yielding to the Ifs can slow us down. If you are hearing a lot of *Ifs* from someone, there's a big, big challenge—and it's caused by *them* stepping on some or all of the other Leadership land mines. Pay attention to these land mines, no doubt about it, they are serious to the *True Leader*. By this point, the negative person is just about blasted away from all the destruction from these land mines, and the deep wounds they have self-inflicted are going to be very hard to heal. Here a possible leader is, just about at the crossroads, and it's so sad to see that person nearly history. Stick to the basics!

Summary: Only play the *What if* game if you are positive, dreaming big, and thinking, "*what if* . . . I sponsor 10 people this month?" "*What if* I can make the next level of the compensation plan?"

Result: If you play the *What if* game and want everything to change before you begin to follow the basics, you could be wasting valuable lifetime.

Truth: *True Leaders* are always looking for two to three new people to build into leaders.

Commit Now! "I will watch my thoughts and stick to the basics; no need to look for ways to change the company to fit my needs."

---

7. **Doubt**—If a person has stepped on many or all of the Leadership land mines, the next step is that doubt creeps in. Who do we start doubting? We don't ever doubt *ourselves*. Here's what happens: we start by doubting the program, the products, our Upline and the company. We start seeing that *everything* is wrong at this point—everything but us.

Doubt is a big obstacle. It's the one thing that can destroy our fabulous Network Marketing future and us.

Here's what *True Leaders* concentrate on:

1. belief in the products
2. belief in the company
3. belief in Network Marketing
4. belief in themselves—as enhanced by personal growth and development

Doubt can kill the belief that is necessary to become a *True Leader*. All the water in the world cannot sink a ship unless it gets *inside* of it.

If belief is lost in the first three areas, doubt becomes so serious that we start doubting ourselves. Disaster begins! Self doubt will lead you right back to your old day job and the thinking that that job at the bank, or the hospital, or the factory is the only way to keep on keepin' on—returning to the same situation that you hated—until you're ready to retire. How sad . . . when doubt destroys belief. *True Leaders know* that when doubt tries to creep in doubt will *lose* the battle.

Summary: Do not permit doubt to destroy your belief in a fabulous future.

Result: Doubt can kill your momentum.

Truth: *True Leaders* are always looking for two to three new emerging leaders.

Commit Now! "I will not let doubt creep in!"

---

8. **Not Building Your Belief System**—This can knock you right off the pathway toward success. Get a *strong belief* in all four areas we discussed above in order to solidify Network Marketing success. Weakness in any of those

four areas will greatly diminish your chance to succeed! Belief in the industry and in yourself are the hardest areas to strengthen—it takes work and persistence! It takes a personal growth and development program. Read the books, listen to tapes and attend seminars by those living the lifestyle that you want. Be very careful to whom you listen. We have chosen to listen only to those living the lifestyle we wanted, not the wannabes, not the false leaders.

Summary: Stay focused on building your Network Marketing business.

Results: Book by book, seminar by seminar, tape by tape, you will begin to feel your belief strengthen as you watch your organization multiply and grow beyond your wildest expectations—as *you* grow beyond who you used to be.

Truth: *True Leaders* are always building belief and looking for two to three emerging leaders.

Commit Today! "I will have belief in myself, in this industry, in my products and in my company. I will take personal responsibility for my Network Marketing success. I will listen to those who are living the lifestyle I desire."

---

9. **Not Using Your Company's Products or Services—** Become a devoted user of your company's services or products! Be your own best customer. When you use your company's products, you can give sincere testimonies. Sincerity is so important in leadership. Know your product, inside, outside and in your sleep. Be able to sell your products with no catalog, photo of them or product in hand. Enthusiastically endorse your own products or services.

Summary: Be your own best customer

Result: People will see you are proud of your product and are seriously committed.

Truth: *True Leaders* are always looking for two to three emerging leaders.

Commit Now! "I will be my own best customer!"

---

10. **Not Feeding Your Mind By Attending the Right Training, Personal Growth and Development Seminars and Company Events that are led by the True Leaders—** Readers are leaders and leaders are readers, no doubt about it. Stepping on this land mine cripples your belief building ability in all four areas that *True Leaders* focus on: company, product, industry and themselves.

Summary: The right events are important to attend.

Result: You might miss the one piece of the puzzle that you need to be a *True Leader*.

Truth: *True Leaders* feed their minds—great stuff in, great stuff out! *True Leaders* are always looking for two to three emerging leaders.

Commit Now! "I will attend the right events and I will feed my mind!"

---

11. **Not Accessing the Upline's and Best Available Support Systems—**New Distributor kits, Upline support, three-way calls, teleconferencing calls, and any connection with the Upline who is making the money. This land mine can cripple confidence. The belief system always needs rebuilding and reinforcing. Not using the company support tools is like going into battle *naked with No weapons!* You are a lot less likely to become a *True Leader* unless

you take advantage of all the business support system possibilities that abound. Do not block information that can flow to you and your team from the Upline that is making the money. Get the best tools available and use them. Search for them. Take massive action when you find the ones that work for you.

Summary: Use the business tools and support systems—take advantage of them.

Result: You will not be seen as trying to control what the new distributor needs—let them discover all the great information and support that is available to them.

Truth: *True Leaders* are always looking for two to three emerging leaders.

Commit Now! "I will take advantage of my Upline and the Network Marketing tools and support provided by this industry and my company!"

---

12. **Thinking You Need To Reinvent the Wheel**— Reinventing any system or tool already in place kills your productivity. Why? Because it takes time and energy away from the most productive activities. After a company is a few years old, leaders and the company have already put some strong tools and systems in place that are working. Use them. If tools have obviously worked for successful distributors already, chances are strong they will work for you too—*if* you access and USE them!

Summary: Use the Upline and tools that are getting results.

Result: *You* will begin to see the same results that the *successful* distributors see.

Truth: *True Leaders* are always looking for two to three emerging leaders.

> **Commit Now!** "I will not attempt to reinvent the wheel!"

13. **Having A Negative Attitude**—The negative energy you put out will actually cause you to *repel* those you may seek to prospect. No one wants to be around a sourpuss and have all *their* precious energy sucked out of them by someone who is always negative! Your attitude determines your altitude. Will you soar or sink?

Summary: *True Leaders* work on having a positive attitude. They know that attitude is really a matter of choice, so they *choose* to *be* positive.

Results: You will attract positive people.

Truth: *True Leaders* are always looking for two to three emerging leaders. Emerging leaders are *attracted* to positive people!

> **Commit Now!** "I will choose to have a positive attitude!"

14. **Not Making A List Of Prospects**—When you are brand new in this business, you can become very apprehensive when the first few people that have come to mind say "no thanks" or "not now." *Then*, where do you go? Who is left to talk to? With a *long* list of 100-200 names, it is no big deal if you get rejected a few times—especially in the beginning—because you have a lot more people right there *on the list* whom you haven't approached yet.

True Leaders work on mastering the effective language and concepts of great presentations. They master the skills of inviting others to look at what they are offering. So they reduce rejection, and they don't let rejection slow them down.

Summary: Start making a long list of people to contact.

Results: When you get rejected you still have more people to contact.

Truth: *True Leaders* are always looking for two to three emerging leaders. The *longer* their prospect list is, the more leaders they will find to grow their group!

Commit Today! "I will follow the pioneers in my company."

---

15. **Not Following Up!**—Stepping on *this* land mine will cause your business to fizzle fast. *Follow-up* is where your fortune is made—*or* where it's lost! Follow up. Hard to do? Sure—often it is. What's hard to do is also easy to do. Worth doing? You bet!

Get organized, have a system that works for you for remembering who to call back and when. Take notes on what was said, what your prospects' interests are, their goals, what they want from their new home-based business. Follow up discussions help you understand what their challenges might be and what support systems they will need most. Learn what to say—sincerely and smoothly—so that your prospects will realize how valuable it will be for them to join into partnership with you and your company. You can do this all with a spiral notebook and telephone and/or a computer. Bottom line— you must stay in touch.

Prospecting and sponsoring is a *process*, not an event. Prospects very rarely say "Yes" after a first exposure to your offering. Often the timing is not quite right just then. They have to be moved "through the pipeline" by being presented with influential information and getting their questions answered. This process is moved along by your follow-ups. Until prospects realize how valuable what you are offering really is *for them*, they are not going to join you. Follow up is the key. Without your follow up, they will go away—maybe to get landed by someone who is more conscientious than you and who *does* do their follow up. Hmmm—what can follow up be worth? Everything!

Summary: Follow up leads to success.

Results: You will be a whole lot more successful—and you will create a more successful culture of following up and doing things right in your whole organization.

Truth: *True Leaders* follow up to find and sponsor those two to three emerging leaders.

Commit Today! "I will get organized and follow up!"

---

16. **Not Being Teachable or Coachable**—It's a lot harder to *be* a pioneer than to follow one. If your company or Upline is already successful, there is a solid path to follow that others have already lain down. Learn from the mistakes of others, so *you* don't have to waste *your* time, energy, money, and reputation making the same mistakes others have already made and have now learned how to avoid!

Summary: Follow and learn from those who are making the money in your organization. Seek them out.

Results: You will begin to see abundance flowing your way.

Truth: *True Leaders* are always learning how to get better, stronger and more effective so their search for those two to three emerging leaders will succeed sooner!

Commit Today! "I will follow and learn from the pioneers in my company."

---

17. **Following the "False" Cubic Zirconia Leader**—A huge mistake! This land mine is usually stepped on by people with a weak sense of self-esteem, and these followers are easily swayed by glitz, glamour, humor, wittiness and the domineering personality of some "false" leader with a *big* ego. There is nothing wrong with having a big ego, as long as it is kept "in check." Sometimes, though, the insatiable thirst big egos have for attention, praise and recognition can eventually be a turn off for many people.

Big egos think they "know it all," and so they are often very poor students and have a very unrealistic sense of how shallow and weak their own knowledge really is. They often lead their followers in the wrong direction, towards the wrong goals with the wrong tools and support systems. They are normally gossips, hypocrites and certainly not people whom we have chosen to pay any attention to. We sought out the people living the lifestyle we wanted, not the recognition seekers. After all, those merely seeking recognition normally leave and go to another company after they build one or two leaders under them. Our experience is that no one has built to the Diamond level.

Strong egos are necessary to survive. That strength will provide the stamina and self-motivation to *keep on going* and get the job done. The strong ego can overcome challenges, and navigate through tough times, yet keep things in perspective. But a big ego out of control and running amok can kill your momentum and organization! If you choose to follow a leader like that, you won't find great success at their destination.

Summary: Find *True Leaders*—learn how to follow them, then become one.

Results: You will begin to see abundance flowing your way, and you'll enjoy the company of the quality people who join you on the path *True Leaders* take.

Truth: *True Leaders* have *strong* egos, not big ones, and they lead in the right direction in the right way—the straightest path toward success!

Commit Today! "I will only follow *True Leaders*, and I will learn how to become one myself!"

---

18. **Failing to be Aware of and Staying Ahead of Trends**— We have found that there are three major trends that make Network Marketing very attractive.

 At-home businesses are a huge trend. Interestingly enough, in the beginning of the 21st century, a new home-based business is created every 10 seconds. And even more exciting is that 96% of adults, over age 25, are looking to own their own business. This strong trend fuels the success of other relatively new businesses like Staples, Office Depot, Office Max and other businesses globally. The relatively low price of computers, printers, fax machines, lower long-distance phone costs, cell phones, e-mail and the Internet have all contributed to this trend.

 A second huge trend is **shopping at home.**

 Many consumers are exhausted from the frantic pace of their lives—long commutes, long hours at the office, taking children to extra curricular activities and trying to do it all. They are looking to buy what they need more easily—from the comfort of their homes. Catalogue sales and mail order first facilitated this trend, then ordering on toll-free phone lines and shopping online over the Internet. Give a credit card number and get products delivered—a huge timesaving! Many people want first class consideration and not the hassle of having to go to a crowded shopping mall, with parking headaches, and poor customer service.

The third huge trend is **the distribution opportunity of Network Marketing. It's a great way products move into the marketplace.** Products used to move much more slowly through a complicated distribution chain. Manufacturers sold their products to a middle man who would resell the products to a wholesaler, who would resell it again to a retailer, who would store it in a warehouse. Later, it would move to a store, where it would go onto a shelf waiting for the customer to hopefully come along and buy it for the third time.

A long time ago, that system made sense. With today's high-speed, worldwide air freight, communications, toll-free ordering, fax lines, Internet ordering, credit cards and speedy UPS and FedEx deliveries, that old system no longer is necessary. Today, a Network Marketing company manufactures a product, ships it direct to the distributor—who in many cases is the end consumer or, in other cases, they market that product to a friend, neighbor or relative. And all those middlemen, who used to collect a piece of the final price as their profit, are gone— no longer necessary.

The result is that it frees up a lot of money. And all this new money that used to get wasted in the old, expanded distribution process, is now going into two key areas for Network Marketing companies: (1) product research and development to create cutting-edge, state-of-the-art products that possibly would not have made it to the marketplace any other way; and (2) to pay the field distributors who are actually doing the diligent, creative marketing work by being energetic advocates of the unique products. Many of these products are not well known. They still need their benefits explained with passion and conviction—conversational marketing.

No distribution channel accomplishes that better than Network Marketing. Obviously, this is the business most able to capitalize on *all* these trends: working at home, shopping from home and the means to capture a huge share of the money that used to flow to all the middlemen in the old distribution chain. Network Marketing has streamlined the distribution of products and services.

Summary: Stay alert to the key trends shaping the world today. Learn how to effectively educate your team members and new prospects on how and why Network Marketing is actually in the best position to capitalize on all these trends.

Result: Your business will grow faster, increasing in strength and stability. Your income will grow and be more stable because incomes of your key leaders will grow as well.

Truth: *True Leaders* seek to understand the world in which their business operates and they know the vital importance of teaching their team how to capitalize on trends.

Commit Now! "I will stay alert to what the trends are and how they affect my business, and I'll teach my team how to capitalize on them."

---

19. **Not Studying Prosperity Principles**—If you truly want to achieve better health, wealth, happiness, have great relationships, drive fabulous cars, wear nice clothes, live in a beautiful home, go on great vacations and have the lifestyle—study people who have already accomplished those prosperous achievements! Learn how *they* did it. What activities and behaviors did they learn and follow to become prosperous?

With Network Marketing, not only do we have unlimited income potential, unlike with any other profession, we have the ability to become successful while helping others achieve success as well! In fact, that is the only way in Network Marketing to get to the top: help enough other people get what they want, and you will bolt to the top of your compensation plan!

Two prosperity principles stand out over all the others.

Get yourself into a position to be a True Leader. For those of you who seek financial independence, an 8-5 job will keep you at just that J. O. B. (Just Over Broke) With almost any job, your boss will buy your services and skills at wholesale and sell them at retail. That's just how business works. The business owner must make a profit off of you. Can *you* get wealthy in that scenario? It's very, very unlikely.

In Network Marketing you can *be* a leader that grows a business to enormous heights. You will have the support of a multi-million dollar company behind you plus all the training, expertise, guidance of your entire successline—with all of those support resources having a vested interest in your success.

If you own a traditional small business, you don't own the business, the business owns *you*. You're fully responsible for its success and for always paying your employees, ordering and paying suppliers for products and on and on.

To even get into a *franchise* today, you need at least 30 thousand dollars on up to over a million dollars to get fully set up—depending on which franchise. And for all that money, you are likely to have bought yourself a minimum wage job. Why? Because while most franchises often make a profit, the business owner will need to be there—*tied to the business*—for 80 or more hours per week; while the employees will be going home after only 40 hours per week.

The second prosperity principle is the principle of Leverage. All regular businesses and jobs have one fatal flaw: they are all part of the trading time for money trap. In this common set up, it's all linear income: you work for 8 hours, so you get paid for 8 hours. If you're sick for half a day, you only get paid for 4 hours; if you miss a day, you don't get paid at all. If you're not there working—for any reason—you don't get paid. Period.

What we have with Network Marketing is *leverage.* We have the ability to create true residual income. Residual income is income that continues to flow even when you are not actively working the business. In creating residual income, you are no longer trading time directly for money. Instead we're creating a flow of income by doing something once, the right way—building a solid, empowered successline, and getting paid on it . . . forever!

True prosperity flows from our understanding and living by the spiritual laws which govern our world. While they don't need to be mastered in your first 90-120 days of your Network Marketing business, the sooner they are studied and applied, the better.

Here are some of the tips we have learned:

Basic prosperity truths: It's great to desire prosperity. Poverty is a sin; prosperity is your divine heritage. There's a link between thought and supply. Success embraces the prosperous attitude.

The basic prosperity law: There's no free lunch; you cannot get something for nothing. You can always give something—even a smile! Radiate and you will attract. Before you can achieve personal financial success, personal growth and development must take place.

The vacuum law of prosperity: Let go of much of what you have accumulated by selling or giving away that which clutters and clogs your life or surroundings. Create a vacuum so something better has room to flow into your life and home.

The creative law of prosperity: Strong desire is success power. Know your "why"—your reasons for wanting success. When the why gets clear, the how gets easy. Prosperity results from planning.

The imaging law of prosperity: Visualize. Success is first created mentally. Persist in picturing success. Imagine your dreams and desires. Paint a mental picture and help others to visualize their dream.

The prosperity law of affirmations: Using positive affirmations through words can solve challenges and make your world better—even wonderful! Read positive affirmations daily.

The prosperity law of increase: Think thoughts of increase. Focus on abundant concepts, not on "hard times." Free yourself from petty thinking. Conquer discouragement and disappointment.

Work is a mighty channel for prosperity: Attitudes make all the difference. Direct your energies toward great goals (NetWORK Marketing—not netMESS-AROUND!). Work is divine. Expect changes for the better. Luck is spelled W. O. R. K.

The prosperity law of love and good will: Turning love on can bring victorious results and healing. Future *True Leaders* thrive on encouragement. Be able to bless and release those who do not want your love.

Your genius powers for prosperity: Genius powers are in you already. Develop and trust your intuition. Sometimes silence is necessary—never underestimate the power of quietness. Self-confidence develops when you focus on your own God given talents.

The prosperity law of self-confidence: Self-confidence is necessary to succeed. Associate with self-confident people. There is power in speaking words of praise. Self-confidence conquers doubt and dissolves inferiority. Do not crave recognition. Be the one who gives it, every day, every way.

The prosperity law of charisma: Charisma is ageless and it's a challenge-solver. Charisma is kindness, and it pays huge dividends. (In Network Marketing you either come in nice, get nice, or get out! Mean, selfish, hypocritical people are seldom successful.) Overcome the destructiveness of gossip—it can subconsciously stop your good. Run the other direction from the gossip. And know this, there are always two sides to the story, check out all the facts before you follow the one who gossips.

The prosperity law of persistence: Your attitude determines your altitude. Never surrender to defeat. Never give up. Persistence produces success. Failures—often repeated failures—can be a prelude to success. Don't look back, look forward. Be prepared for success. Persistence and tenacity are all-powerful. One way to learn how to do something right, do it wrong. The definition of insanity is doing something over and over hoping to get different results. If what you are doing is not working, stop, take notice and try a different approach.

It's easier to follow a pioneer than to be one. Studying how others have achieved prosperity will reap valuable tips that will help you soar.

Summary: To become prosperous, start by studying leadership and putting the principle of leverage to work.

Result: More prosperity will flow to you, and your income will be more secure as you teach these valuable principles to others.

Truth: *True Leaders* study how others have achieved prosperity so they learn the valuable tips needed to get there sooner, and then they teach these to their team.

> **Commit Now!** "I will study, learn and teach the prosperity principles."

20. **Not crafting your vision**—Building a big successline organization starts with building a big vision. We all begin small and alone in building our Network Marketing business, and when you expand your vision of the size, depth and strength of your team, it will grow and expand like wildfire.

    True Leaders have vision. They think and plan for years in advance. They are always thinking about the future.

    Many people in Network Marketing have limits on their vision because they only see what they have seen and experienced in the past. They limit themselves to the narrow scope of their own past personal experiences. Too often, they expect too little, so they don't get much. You get what you expect.

    You already have a vision. Your vision itself is free, and you can change it whenever you want to. Your success is up to you.

    Take a moment to flip to the front of this book, and reread the quote from Nelson Mandella's 1994 inaugural speech. His is an enormous vision that encompasses every one of us! That's the scope of vision *True Leaders* have for their entire organization. It can be very empowering and inspiring, but for many aspiring leaders, big vision doesn't just happen—it must be crafted.

How do you craft your vision? Work on self-development and learning the techniques and enormous value of envisioning success. The rewards are huge. You will be able to empower others to create big visions of their own, eliminating bad habits by shattering the beliefs which cause them, creating positive thought patterns, staying self-motivated and fired up, and achieving your goals and dreams!

A very helpful resource includes the "Crafting Your Vision" tape album featuring visionary insights from Jan Ruhe (available from www.janruhe.com).

Summary: Building a big, successful Network Marketing team starts with building a bigger vision. The rewards of diligently crafting your vision can be huge!

Result: Your business will boom, your organization will be strong and prosperous—and so will you!

Truth: *True Leaders* are visionaries. They see beyond the invisible. They have the ability to take the time to see into the future.

Commit Now! "I will craft my vision so that it's big enough to encompass my dreams and the dreams of my entire team."

---

21. **Not building your dreams**—Accomplishing the escape from a life of quiet desperation to a fantastic, abundant life of financial independence, personal independence, a life of meaning, purpose, fulfillment and contribution will happen when you put yourself into the role of always being the student. Achieving control of your own destiny

happens for those of you who are self-motivated and who are engaged on the path of personal growth and development, developing skills in communications and building your successline. When you have the right vehicle (a sound company) and a real *passion* for making your dreams come true, have stickability and never let anyone kill your dreams, no doubt, you will achieve greatness!

Why? With passion for achieving your dreams, people will *find* that they will love being in this business.

"There is a day that you get into Network Marketing, but nothing happens until the day that Network Marketing gets into you."
~ Jan Ruhe

You will have the self-motivation required to take massive *actions* that will be productive and get you on to an ascending fast track to success. Breathing LIFE back into "lost" dreams is *critical* to success in our business.

Think back to when you were younger—what were your dreams then? Children are so resilient—so many children dream about when they grow up they are going to be an astronaut, a rock star, a sports star, or a leader in politics, doctor, lawyer, actor, etc. And what *really* happens along the way? They get out of high school or college and get into their first job. Is it their dream job? Not usually, but they take it to get going. Then bills pile up, debt grows, obligations mount—and their income seldom increases at the same pace.

They may get married. Children come along with diapers to buy and higher food bills, and they need new shoes about every three months—then braces and piano lessons or other activities. And does income grow enough to handle all these new bills? Not likely. Debt grows. And what happens to all those vivid dreams of so long ago? Too often, they get shoved into the background and sometimes even crushed by "reality." Those beautiful dreams just kind of *die* . . . so sad, isn't it?

What were *your* dreams as you turned twenty, or when you first got married? What kind of car did you want to drive? What kind of home did you want to live in? Where? What kind of vacations did you dream of taking? What kind of income is needed to make that all possible?

Think quietly right now—about your dreams and desires today. What are the five things that you would do, have or become, if money was no object? Make a Master Dream list.

Now, ask yourself: Are you on track today, in your present job, to achieve the income to enable your dreams? Do you think others with aspirations like yours are on track? Perhaps a second income would be so very attractive. Money provides freedom. It gives you choices. For many of us, all over the world, money is right up there in importance with oxygen!

Way too many people conclude at first that they are "too busy" to fit Network Marketing into their tight schedule. Yet when you help them look honestly at their situation, it turns out that they are actually busy being broke. They are stuck in the rat race without sufficiently increasing income. If you help them get in touch with their dreams again, they are much more likely to find those 7 to 10 hours a week that they will need to join your Network Marketing team and build a second income stream—so they can finally achieve their dreams! They need you to help them understand why the opportunity Network Marketing creates is so appealing to those who understand its potential: unlimited income—and a chance to finally turn those "lost" dreams into reality!

Summary: Refocusing on your dreams and feeding your mind will nurture your imagination and rekindle that deep longing for ultimately achieving your dreams.

Result: You will develop that special, dynamic energy necessary to spark your self-motivation. Then you can engage in the actions required to drive your business to such successful levels that achievement of your dreams will be possible!

Truth: *True Leaders* pursue their dreams with a passion!

Commit Now! "I will build my dreams and achieve them! I will let no one kill my dreams"

Final Thoughts

It's okay to make a few mistakes and step on a land mine every now and then. We can all heal from small, occasional wounds, but if land mines explode underneath you too often, after a while, you get so mangled that you can't continue doing the business—*you* just explode too—you get blown away. By reading this book, you are already *way ahead* of most Network Marketers! Congratulations!

Recognize these land mines. Be aware of when you are stepping on them, so you can teach and guide others on how to *avoid* them, step around them and stay solidly on the safest pathway toward success. How? Consult with your successful Upline, and seek to see the biggest picture—so you can spot when you're wandering off the pathway to success and into the minefield.

Guide others around these land mines and help them learn *how* to recognize them, so they can teach the people on their teams these same skills so they won't get destroyed. That's the job of the *True Leader—to be an excellent Guide*.

We believe in you. We want you to avoid these land mines.

"We wish you wealth, health, happiness. A life in which you give to yourself the gift of patience, the virtue of reason, the value of knowledge and the influence of faith in your own ability to dream about and to achieve worthy rewards."
~ Jim Rohn

And we wish you great Network Marketing *and True Leadership* success!

Chapter 5

True Leadership Stories

❧ THE TRUTH ABOUT GEESE ☙

HAVE YOU EVER WONDERED WHY GEESE FLY IN A "V" formation? Here are some interesting facts scientists have discovered about why they fly that way.

Fact: As each bird flaps its wings, it creates uplift for the bird immediately following. By flying in a "V" formation, the whole flock adds at least 71% greater flying range than if each bird flew on its own.

Truth: People who share a common direction and sense of community can get where they are going quicker and easier because they are traveling on the trust of one another.

Fact: Whenever a goose falls out of formation, it suddenly feels the drag and resistance of trying to go it alone and quickly gets back into formation to take advantage of the lifting power of the bird immediately in front.

Truth: There is strength and power and safety in numbers when traveling in the same direction with those with whom we share a common goal.

Fact: When the lead goose gets tired, it rotates back in the V formation and another goose flies point.

Truth: Each of us needs to take our turn in giving direction for the good of the whole.

Fact: The geese honk from behind to encourage those up front to keep up their speed.
Truth: We all need to be remembered and stimulated with active support and praise.

Fact: When a goose gets sick or is wounded and falls out, two geese fall out of formation and follow it down to help and protect it. They stay with it until the crisis resolves, and then they launch out on their own or with another formation to catch up with their group.
Truth: We must stand by each other in times of need. We are fortunate that there are more geese in life than turkeys. Let's remember to uphold each other in friendship and to give each other a big "honk" more often.

~ Adapted from Angeles Arrien

❦ THE DONKEY STORY ❧

A PARABLE IS TOLD OF A FARMER WHO OWNED AN OLD, worn-out, tired mule. The mule had not worked hard for quite some time. The farmer just didn't think it was worth keeping and feeding such a useless animal. One day the mule fell into the farmer's well. It was a long fall. The farmer assumed that the donkey was gone.

The farmer heard the mule braying—or whatever mules do when they fall into wells. After carefully assessing the situation, the farmer sympathized with the mule, but decided that neither the mule nor the well was worth the trouble of saving. So, he called his neighbors together and told them what had happened . . . and enlisted them to help haul dirt to bury the old mule in the well and put it out of its misery!

Shovel upon shovel of dirt began to hit the old, tired mule's back. Initially, the old mule was hysterical, but as the farmer and his neighbors continued shoveling and the dirt hit his back . . . a thought struck the mule! It suddenly dawned on him that every time a shovel load of dirt landed on his back . . . he should simply

shake it off and step up!

This he did, blow after blow. **Shake it off and step up . . . shake it off and step up . . . shake it off and step up!"**

He kept repeating this to encourage himself. He got a vision that he could survive. He would survive. He knew it. No matter how painful the blows, or distressing the situation seemed, the old mule fought "panic" and just kept right on . . .

shaking it off and stepping up!

It wasn't long before the old mule, battered and exhausted, *stepped triumphantly over the wall of that well!* He had survived, just like he knew he would. He did not let all that dirt bury him and make him give up . . . no, he shook off the dirt and stepped up, just like *True Leaders* do. What seemed like it would *bury him* actually *blessed him . . . all because of the manner* in which he *handled his adversity!*

That's life! If we face our challenges and respond to them positively, and refuse to give in to panic, bitterness, to the critics, to the hypocrites, to those who hurt us, disappoint us, or to situations beyond our control, or self-pity . . .

the adversities that come along to bury us usually have within them the potential to benefit and bless us!

⊰ The Little Burro Story ⊱

IN THE OLD DAYS OUT WEST, RANCHERS WOULD SOME-times take a wild steed that they could not break, tie it to a little burro, and turn the two loose. The steed would rear up on its hind legs snorting defiance, irritated beyond belief, distracted, and unhappy. Off they would go, out onto the range. Before long the bucking steed would disappear over the desert horizon, dragging the helpless burro behind.

Days would pass, but eventually the odd couple would reappear. The little burro would come first, with the submissive steed in tow.

What went on out on the range always brought *the same result*. The steed would buck and kick and pitch and pull, but the burro, willing or not, would

hang on, no matter what.

Finally, the steed would become exhausted, and at that point the burro would take over and

become the leader.

That's the way it is in life.

True Leaders hang on.

They are the determined, the committed. They know that perseverance can bring them out on top. No matter what . . .

Hang on.
Do not give up on your dreams.

True Leaders dream big. They get a plan, a vision, and a system that works over and over again and they seek out those who are living the lifestyle they want and make a decision to decide to go for it, no matter what. They get a plan, plan to work and work their plan. No matter what, they hang on to their convictions and are strong enough to take on the steeds. They have patience to handle those greater than them. They hang on and accomplish great feats, and build success upon success.

It's the journey. It's who you become when you arrive at being a *True Leader* that is what makes the hanging on so important. Begin today to get a plan, read the books, get involved in your own personal growth and development program. When you are at the end of your rope, tie a knot in it and hang on. When you are ready to quit, that's the time to start all over again. Remember the little burro.

"When you are through changing, you're through."

~ Bruce Barton

⋟ THE WOLF STORY ⋞

ALL OF US KNOW WHAT IT'S LIKE TO BE ATTACKED BY painful feelings, thoughts, hypocrites, unkind words, gossip, false accusations, those who should but don't and won't recognize our contributions, those who try to conquer and divide, those who break promises, disappoint us and worst of all—the critics. Have you ever wondered why these mental and emotional challenges cling so persistently or if it's possible to break their grip? Here is the answer.

Suppose a stranger came to your front door leading a *vicious* wolf on a chain. He states:

"I believe this is your wolf."

You would quickly reply that *the wolf does not belong in your home.*

Wolves of dread, doubt, worry, loneliness *do not belong in your life.* Our mistake can be that we identify with people, situations and inner conditions. When we *identify* that means that we take things to be a part of *our* identity, which they truly are *not.* They exist only because we do not realize our true nature. A person who thinks he is his wealth will worry over losing it. A person who depends on relatives to make them feel needed and appreciated will be anxious over offending them.

When attacked by a wolf of any kind, *you must reply* with deep *wisdom and passion and conviction,*

"Regardless of how I feel about it, that wolf does not belong to me."

Include *"Regardless of how I feel about it,"* because safe feelings will lie to you for a long time. They want you to think that they belong to you, for their treacherous existence depends upon you believing their false claim. Make them disappear forever. **Beware.** *Do not let the wolf into your life!*

True Leaders understand this.

⌒

"Great things are not done by impulse but by a series of small things brought together."

~ Vincent Van Gogh

❧ THE FROGS ❧

A GROUP OF FROGS WERE TRAVELING THROUGH THE woods, and two of them fell into a deep, dark and scary pit. All the other frogs gathered around the pit. When they saw how deep the pit was, they told the two frogs that they were as good as dead. The two frogs in the pit ignored the comments and tried to jump out of the pit with all of their might.

The other frogs kept telling them to stop trying, to quit jumping and give in, that they were as good as dead.

Finally, one of the two frogs in the pit heard what the other frogs were saying. He believed them, paid attention and followed their pleas. He decided he couldn't keep jumping. It wasn't worth it; he gave up, and died.

However, the other frog continued to jump and jump and jump, banging himself against the walls. He was determined to get out, no matter what. He jumped and jumped and just knew that he *could* and would get out. His vision of what would happen was clear. He would not be denied. He couldn't hear the other frogs, even though they were yelling at him.

The crowd of frogs continued to yell at him to stop the pain, quit jumping, just give in and die. Not this frog, no way, he was a champion frog and he knew it, he would survive, no doubt about it! He jumped even harder and *finally* jumped out of the pit. When he got out, the other frogs said, "Didn't you hear us? We never believed you would make it out alive. We thought for sure you would give up and die!"

The frog explained to them that he was deaf. He never heard them encouraging him to give in. *He* thought they were encouraging him to jump *out* the entire time.

There is power of life and death in the tongue!

An encouraging word to someone who is down can lift them up and help them make it through the day. You never know how your words will impact someone else. Your words are powerful. Your cheering on someone to succeed is the most important gift you can give someone. People need to hear you cheer them on, not tell them to give up on their dreams. And mostly when people are down, they are struggling to get out of the pits that sometimes life brings us. It's so wonderful to be around people who are champions, who cheer for you and pick you up when you are down. They are rare; they are the *True Leaders*.

A destructive word to someone who is down can be all that's needed to kill their dream. *Be careful of what you say.* Think before you speak. Turn a deaf ear to those who tell you that you can't make it. Because the truth is, you can. There has never been a better time to set your sights on becoming a *True Leader*.

True Leaders are emerging all over the world. There has never been a better time to be alive and thrive! When you think of saying anything discouraging, think and *remember the frogs.*

Speak *belief* in others, encourage them and tell them not to give in, but to press on. Never *give up* on your dreams. Dream big, get the vision, your dreams are going to see you through! Somewhere there is a road map of how to reach your destination.

The power of words . . . it is sometimes hard to understand that an encouraging word can go such a long way. Anyone can speak words that tend to rob another of the spirit to continue in difficult times. Special is the individual who will take the time to encourage another. Be considerate to others. Watch your words. Be the one cheering others on to greatness. The *True Leader* does.

⌒

"A.B.C.—Always Be Complete.
Remember this when designing your business and your life. Because every detail you leave out must be filled in by someone else."
~ Michael S. Clouse

❧ THE GUIDE ☙

I N THE SUMMER OF 1998, JAN TOOK HER FAMILY ON A relaxing three-hour canoe trip. She had a picnic catered for them and took two canoes through Independence Pass, up into the mountains from Aspen, Colorado. Just glorious! It was somewhat overcast so it wasn't hot and the river was very peaceful.

Their private guide was great. He had been a CEO of a huge corporation and walked out of his office seven years ago, moved to Aspen, became a guide on the river—and he never looked back!

He said some interesting things:
- When you are a guide, you have been through the course a thousand times.
- You never know who you are guiding. He had been the guide for the great actor, Kevin Costner, the day before.
- Your customer service must be at 100% at all times.
- When you are on the river **you have to:**
  - navigate around obstacles.
  - back-paddle to change course in the direction you are going.
  - have courage to keep going sometimes.
  - paddle to get going.
  - keep doing the basic things over and over.

You must:
- **be able** to cater to all kinds of personalities.
- **be ready, upbeat, enthusiastic** and **show** that you love what you are doing.
- **give your best guidance** every time you go out on the river.

♦ **not let** the river control you. **You** are in control.

You mainly get new clients by word of mouth. If you do a great job, your customers will tell others. If you do a bad job, your customers will pass that along too.

"True Leaders know that people thrive on the appreciation you show them, the smiles, the thanks and the gestures of kindness."

~ Anonymous

✺ THE BEGINNING OF MERCEDES BENZ ✺

I N 1886, KARL BENZ PROUDLY DROVE HIS FIRST AUTOMO-bile through the streets of Munich, Germany. The car was the forerunner of today's Mercedes Benz.

The machine angered the citizens, because it was noisy and scared the children and horses. People criticized him, were upset with him, gossiped about him, were rude toward him, did not take an interest in his product, shunned him, complained about him to the authorities, became meanspirited, were unpleasant and put out.

Pressured by the citizens, the local officials immediately established a speed limit for horse-less carriages of 3½ miles per hour inside the city limits and 7 miles per hour outside.

Benz knew he could never develop a market for his car and compete against horses if he had to creep along at those speeds, so he invited the mayor of the town for a ride. Smart move. The mayor accepted. Benz then arranged for a milk-man to park his horse and wagon on a certain street and, as Benz and the mayor drove by, the milkman whipped up his old horse, as planned, and passed them—rudely gesturing with the German equivalent of the Bronx cheer as he trotted by.

The plan worked. The mayor was furious and demanded that Benz overtake the milk wagon. Benz apologized but said that because of the ridiculous speed law he was not permitted to go any faster. Would you be surprised to hear that . . . *very soon after the law was changed? The speed limit was lifted for Benz.*

Why? Because Benz proved that the art of diplomacy and leadership is getting people to see things *your* way. He did not fight those nasty people who tried to block his idea. He came up with a plan to include and educate a *decision-maker*. The mayor was smart; he accepted the invitation although so many people had complained. The mayor was fair. He sought to understand Benz and his new machine.

True Leaders are smart and fair; they don't just listen to those who complain and gossip about others. They go for the ride and normally find out there is more to see than just the critics' side. *Do not give up on your dreams!*

Interestingly enough, Jan traveled to Switzerland in early 2000 to view this car in a museum there.

"If you think you can, or you think you can't you're probably right."
~ Mark Twain

❧ THE SUCCESS STORY
OF BETTY SUNG ❧

RENE REID YARNELL

B ORN IN TAIPEI, TAIWAN AND IMMIGRATING TO
America, Betty Sung is the living testimonial of an emerging
leader. As the third girl born to her Chinese parents, she grew
up with the constant reminder that she was the "son" her parents could never have. Because of her childhood, Betty grew
up with a determination to build her inner strength. Through
marriage, she migrated to the United States in 1972, where
she hoped the change would improve her plight.

In the early years, Betty's arrival in the States was anything but the American dream. Speaking little English and
lacking the skills valued most in the marketplace, she was
forced to take almost any job she could find to support her
child and husband, who was on an academic scholarship.
Because the pay was so inadequate, Betty usually worked
three jobs simultaneously. She says softly, reflecting back on
that period of her life, "It was a very tough time for me. So
when a friend introduced me to Network Marketing, I began
to compare this with what I was doing. I learned that, for the
first time, I had the chance to leverage my income by leverag-
ing my time."

Through the Networking industry, Betty saw the potential to explore her leadership skills. A year after joining our
company, she had already attained the distinction of reaching
the highest pay level. In time, Betty began traveling to Asia to

help the company expand internationally. Through hard work, self-discipline, leading by example, assuming responsibility for her group, and respecting each person in her group, Betty built one of the largest Network Marketing organizations in the world!

Betty teaches her people what she considers to be the true meaning of Network Marketing: "Ours is a people business. It is a way to help us change our lives and ourselves. Network Marketing is much more about personal growth than about money. By our example, others will follow suit generating a strong, stable, loyal group of people. And it is through them that we begin to generate a good income."

Betty and her husband grew apart. It was time for her to make another major life transition, this time as a naturalized American single woman. It was during this period of painful transition that she felt she began to make strides in her personal growth: to gain wisdom, to be a better person, to be more positive, and to be more sensitive in sharing these qualities with others who are struggling. By her example, Betty is the epitome of someone who subscribes to ours being a business of building relationships - lifetime relationships. She cares about her people. She truly loves each of them. Throughout her organization, she has generated more than two hundred leaders who have reached the top of the pay plan and are living lives of complete freedom. And this spirit is spreading throughout the several hundred thousand distributors in her worldwide organization expanding to 27 countries.

Although she could live in a mansion or have several homes around the world, she chooses to live humbly in a hotel suite in Taipei. "I try to keep my life simple. If I possess a lot of material things, I don't think I am free to grow in wisdom. The more I can alleviate myself of earthly things, the more I am able to have spiritual freedom. I want to let go of yearning for things and direct my desires toward other more rewarding events. Then I can have the money to pursue the causes I really like to support."

In her worldwide travels, Betty has changed the lives of many people as she goes from country to country working with her primarily Asian groups. She commands a deep respect as a person who is in the process of deepening her wisdom, discovering her serenity, and continually striving to learn and grow as a person. She enjoys the process of traveling and teaching these concepts to others. Betty is the epitome of a *True Leader*.

⌒

"True Leaders have the courage to take action where others hesitate."
~ Anonymous

❧ SNOWBALLS IN JULY ☙

STANLEY ARNOLD WAS A MAN WITH MILLION-DOLLAR ideas. Years ago, Arnold was managing one of his father's 15 Pick-N-Pay stores in Cleveland, Ohio, when a blizzard hit town. The city was paralyzed, and all 15 stores were empty. Employees who had reported to work didn't have much to do—until Arnold came up with his idea.

He had the employees make snowballs—7,900 of them! Then he had the snowballs packed into grapefruit crates and transported to a deep-freeze facility. Then he asked the Weather Bureau when he could expect the hottest day of the year. They told him mid-July. Armed with this information, Arnold took a train to New York and went to see Charles Mortimer, then president of General Foods. He proposed a joint promotional sale of General Food's newly introduced Birds Eye frozen foods. The sale was to be held in mid-July, and young Mr. Arnold wanted General Foods to provide an array of prizes. The sale was to be called "A Blizzard of Values."

As his contribution, Arnold proposed to give away . . . *snowballs*.

General Foods agreed to cooperate. Summer came, and it turned out to be 100 degrees on the sale date. Police had to be called to control the crowds. During the five days of Pick-N-Pay's "Blizzard of Values," some 40,000 General Foods samples were given away, along with 7,900 grapefruit-sized snowballs! Thousands of customers were introduced to the new products, and the food industry discovered what *excitement* could do for sales. All this from a simple, enterprising idea from an employee who cared. The decision-makers at General Foods *listened* to a new and clever idea and *acted* on it. The word about General Foods spread far and wide. Maybe *you* can have your own "Blizzard of Values" event in your own organization? What could that lead to . . . ?

Dream big. Your dreams are going to see you through! Do not give up on your dreams. Go full out and reach them. You can. Success is simply a choice! *True Leaders* know that what sometimes seems like a "wild" idea can be more valuable than you can even imagine!

"Even though you're on the right track-
you'll get run over if you just sit there."
~ Will Rogers

❧ LISTEN TO . . . WHO? ☙

TWO UNEMPLOYED PEOPLE WERE SUNNING THEMSELVES on a park bench. They struck up a conversation.

"The reason I'm here," said one, "is that *I refused to listen* to anyone."

"That's funny," said the other. "I'm here because *I listened to everyone*."

The best course for most of us lies somewhere between the two. We urge you to be careful to whom you listen. We have chosen to listen to those living the lifestyle we want. *True Leaders* receive suggestions from so many people. Many of the ideas will not be usable. There will always be some people in a business or organization who usually offer ideas that are unrealistic and impractical. The *True Leader* has strength and confidence not to be swayed by them.

No one has a monopoly on all the ideas that will be good for an organization. *True Leaders* are always looking for great, new exciting ideas from everyone, not just favorites. What we have found is that we listen and seek to understand from everyone, especially all of our top leaders. The worst mistake that a company can make is to ignore their top leaders. Shame! The bottom line does not lie.

Take special care of the people who help you build your organization more than anyone else. *They* are the ones with the wisdom, experience and the drive to succeed. *True Leaders* understand that they must listen to those actually *living* the lifestyle that *they* are seeking for themselves.

They know that integrity makes a big difference. Really knowing *who* to listen to *and* who to merely smile at will get you where you want to go a lot sooner and with a lot less distraction! *True Leaders* know how smart it is when they choose to turn a deaf ear to those who talk the talk but don't walk the walk.

"A beautiful young person is an accident of nature, but a beautiful old person is a work of art."
~ Eleanor Roosevelt

❧ GET THE RIGHT MAP ☙

A YOUNG MAN ONCE INHERITED A VERY VALUABLE treasure map. The map would guide him to immense wealth and a huge fortune. It was skillfully drawn and it made *very clear* the many trails and trials necessary to go over and through in order to reach the treasure site. He was so excited about this very special map, and even more excited about the treasure.

At the bottom of the old parchment, very faint but still visible, were words to the effect that the treasure could be reached safely but *only by avoiding the dangerous pits and snares* that had been designed to protect it from would-be looters. The map was the key.

And so for many restless days prior to his departure, the young man guarded his secret map closely. He knew that there were many evil characters that were always on the look-out for someone with a real map.

Then, one dark night late in the hour before the dawn of the treasure-seeker's journey, a shape with no shadow stole into his sleeping room. Ever so quietly this thief in the night slipped the real map out from under the man's pillow and slipped back in a clever forgery. In an instant the thief was gone and nothing stirred to tell of his dark visit.

The next morning, when the man awoke, he gathered up his belongings, deliberately tucked the map away in his belt and was on his way. He couldn't help smiling to himself about his good fortune to come, but even this he did with no outward sign, for fear someone should see him and become curious about his happiness.

But his happiness soon faded. He couldn't understand what the challenge could be. Each place on the map that promised safety delivered danger. There were other concerns, too. Almost nothing was where the map said it should be when it said it should be there. A few times he barely escaped with his life.

But the *promise of immense wealth kept him going.* He blamed his consistent confusion and misfortunes on his map-reading ability. He pressed on.

Then one night as he lay awake, unable to sleep under a star-filled sky, he asked himself a question that had been in the back of his mind since the first mishap of the treasure hunt. He didn't really want to permit the question up to the surface of his mind but something within him was crying out for attention. He knew that his recent brushes with near disaster were trying to tell him something, something important. What if his challenge wasn't in the way he was reading the map, but in the map itself? The thought shook him. And yet, he knew it had to be true. All of the evidence was pointing in one direction. No other explanation made sense. The map had to be a phony! *He had been following false directions!*

His humiliation was great but *the lesson was far greater.* Now there was a real choice to be made, perhaps the greatest he would ever have to make. He could give in to his still strong refusal to accept the truth of his situation or he could give up that obviously confused and compulsive part of himself that was still insisting he believe a lie.

He gave up instead of in. He returned to his home. In the years that followed he became one of the world's most successful and longest lived true treasure hunters.

When he was asked (which happened very often) *what*

the key to victory was and how he always knew when there was real treasure to be found, he always smiled and told his secret. He knew that very few would ever understand its special meaning.

"A real treasure map," he would say, "takes work *not* worry to follow."

"If there's worry in the map, there's nothing in the treasure."
~ The True Treasure Hunter

You, too, can have the same self-confidence and total well-being that the treasure-seeker in our story eventually found if you will learn to *welcome self-discovery*. Self-discovery is the key to unlocking the treasure of self-enrichment.

Perhaps you dimly sense, as did our young seeker, that some of what you may discover will be disturbing because it won't confirm your current maps. That should be of no concern to you whatsoever. Giving up self-defeating life demands is as easy as stepping off a down elevator that you had mistakenly thought was going up.

You can see there is nothing more important than this special kind of self-clarity. It is what determines the direction of your life. Choose in favor of yourself. Choose to carefully follow the *True Leader*. Don't use the wrong map!

If Not You, Who . . .

Will write a presentation that grows your team?

Will share a thought that transforms your team?

Will help another person succeed?

Will crack a joke in a meeting that desperately needs one?

Will stop a mistake from happening?

Will uncover a new and important way of leading?

Will be the one to be loyal to the *True Leader*?

Will be the one to not follow the false leader?

Will give fair and well-deserved recognition?

Will strive to help create *True Leaders* and make *them* successful?

Chapter 6

Comparison Charts for True Diamond Leadership!

F IND WHAT YOU ARE DOING RIGHT, AND FIND WHERE YOU need to improve! Go Diamond!

Why not *you* and why not *Now?*

Cubic Zirconia "Leaders":	True Diamond Leaders:
• abuse their power of choice —are not team players.	◆ know they have the **power of choice**.
• act negatively, are unsupportive and disrespectful of their Uplines. They get a title and their big ego kicks in so they begin to gossip.	◆ know that the people who are **positive, supporting and respectful** (part of the solution) are the successful *True Leaders*.
• always make demeaning jokes or wisecracks that belittle others in hopes it will make them look cool.	◆ have the **dignity** and **courtesy** (and good sense!) to be respectful to everyone.
• are stalled by momentary setbacks which take them a long time to settle.	◆ **refuse to be defeated** by momentary setbacks. It's what's finally achieved that really counts.

Cubic Zirconia "Leaders":	True Diamond Leaders:
• need approval from everyone.	♦ **choose to not need** someone *else's* **permission to succeed** —**are courageous** all alone, if necessary.
• promote people and don't teach or train leadership.	♦ **incubate** and **nourish** future leaders.
• qualify themselves based on some achievement in the past.	♦ **continue** to walk the talk— they are genuine.
• question the *True Leaders*.	♦ **question stance** of those with less experience.
• quit for the worst reasons.	♦ **never, never, ever quit!**
• part of the challenge.	♦ part of the **solution** in challenges.
• stingy.	♦ **generous.**
• suspicious.	♦ **trustworthy.**
• swayed more by *facts* than opinions.	♦ **know** that the bottom line doesn't lie.
• the critics.	♦ their **own** best critic.
• very opinionated.	♦ swayed more by **facts** than opinions.

Cubic Zirconia "Leaders" Are Not:	True Diamond Leaders:
• accountable.	♦ are absolutely **accountable.**
• compassionate.	♦ are **compassionate.**
• good examples.	♦ know that they have the **responsibility** to be an *excellent* example, but understand that they are human and not perfect.
• there for you when you are down.	♦ **are there for you** when you are down, troubled or being attacked by the Cubic Zirconias (CZs).
• accepting of constructive criticism.	♦ can **determine** who can accept constructive criticism. They know it'll help make one stronger.
• open to finding what is wrong.	♦ **discover** what is the challenge, **and** they strive to fix it. Sometimes they realize **blessing and releasing** is the best and most healthy decision to the strength of their organization.

Cubic Zirconia "Leaders" Choose to:	True Diamond Leaders:
• complain that they aren't making any money.	♦ **love the journey**—remain remain persistent and courageous!
• create noisy diversions to hide their insecurity.	♦ have the **tenacity** to survive, pick up the pieces, repair what is tarnished and start over.

Cubic Zirconia "Leaders" Choose to:	True Diamond Leaders:
• criticize and whine to anyone who'll listen. If you aren't available, they'll keep looking for anyone who is.	♦ know that **there are no statues erected** to the critics. They don't waste precious life time being the critics. They are able to use their time much more effectively.
• take their focus *off* their own business (because that's *easier* and feeds their ego), and then they complain that they are not making more money.	♦ **choose to succeed**—stay *focused* on creating personal business breakthroughs that accomplish prosperity. They mind their own business.
• dig their high heels in.	♦ combine **tough mindedness** with **flexibility.**
• drink too much alcohol before phoning their colleagues or superiors for help or advice.	♦ **dwell** on their strengths.
• do "their own thing." If they're not the leader on an issue, they try to conquer and divide. They're not there when you need them.	♦ **know** that no real team allows one player license to follow their personal preferences. No coach or team member can *ever* be comfortable wondering if the volatile, untrustworthy, loose cannon teammate will "be there" when they need them most. And they **bless and release** those cannons with ease.
• eliminate opposition.	♦ **don't** try to eliminate opposition unless it is **hurtful to the organization.** Seek to **understand** the scope of issues. If they can't fix it, they bless and release with ease.

Cubic Zirconia "Leaders" Choose to:	True Diamond Leaders:
• digest everything—they succumb to analysis paralysis.	♦ are **impatient**—want to make things happen! They *take action* and *just do it!*
• embarrass others.	♦ aren't **worried about embarrassment**. Know that sometimes they will make the wrong decision and realize they are just human, not perfect.

Cubic Zirconia "Leaders" Don't:	True Diamond Leaders:
• or won't communicate when hurt, angry, confused or off track.	♦ **remain cool** under fire, and they take action when attacked. They are able to **bless and release** easily.
• solve challenges.	♦ **look positively** at challenge—as an opportunity!
• take a stand.	♦ totally **believe** in their proven strategic success track.
• take the actions to become rich.	♦ have a **wealth, abundance and prosperity consciousness** —take the actions required to achieve success.
• have any time when you need them, but if you asked them to count dollar bills and keep all they count, they'd suddenly be free 24 hours a day!	♦ know they must **take a stand** for a better future for their organization. And they know that *investing* time and energy *now* will *pay off* big time later on!

Cubic Zirconia "Leaders" Don't:	True Diamond Leaders:
• know how or who to counsel. Normally make a mess because they don't have all the facts.	♦ **offer counsel** on the best approaches to take. They see a bigger picture by using *all the facts.* Always know that there are two sides to every story.
• show the skill, art and respectful need for apprenticeship.	♦ first *pay the price* as a **good follower, apprentice, helper and student;** and then they *earn* the stature of a master.
• prepare well for their position. They don't build any base or solid foundation.	♦ **prepare well** for their position. Build a solid foundation.
• seek the best solutions.	♦ **point out** possible avenues to a solution.
• work on *building* achievement and confidence in others.	♦ know that **achievement** breeds more confidence, and confidence breeds more **achievement!**
• challenge others.	♦ understand that they must **challenge** people to go where they have never been before.
• read and teach the basics that get results.	♦ understand that a *True Leader* is always also a **student.** School is never out for the *True Leader.*

Cubic Zirconia "Leaders" Usually:	True Diamond Leaders:
• fear change.	♦ don't **allow fear** to prevent them from trying. They feel the fear and do it anyway.
• feel the need to always be happy, enthusiastic and energetic (even if artificially so).	♦ are **tireless, consistent examples of enthusiasm and energy**—and they choose to be that way!
• find a buddy they can control. They foster "Mother Hen Complex" and codependency, which stifles group growth and development of independent leaders.	♦ **choose to associate** with *winners* and nurture future winners in their organization. They **empower** emerging winners to help them gain the skills and independence to fly on their own. And they can let go.
• focus on features.	♦ **First learn prospects' values** (by asking what's important to *them*—by asking questions *and actively listening*), then *tout appropriate* **benefits**—of products, service, company, opportunity and development/support.
• fudge on what they earn.	♦ **never lie** about what they earn.
• get paralyzed and can't make the best decisions. They must digest everything, and they take too long to figure out a workable solution.	♦ **suggest immediate action** that can help bring a challenge or a situation under control.
• get stopped easily.	♦ are **unstoppable.**
• go their own way. Will "reinvent the wheel" in a heartbeat.	♦ go the **proven** way. They **seek, embrace, install** and **use** *duplicable* systems for success.

Cubic Zirconia "Leaders" Usually:	True Diamond Leaders:
• hang with people who are not top performers, and who are critics of those who are.	♦ **hang out** with the movers and shakers! Seek out those who have more wisdom and experience than they do. Choose to follow those who are living the lifestyle they want.
• have excuses why they fail.	♦ **have reasons** why they succeed.
• hold grudges.	♦ are **forgiving.**
• keep trying to change others—unwilling to work on any personal growth.	♦ **embrace** a life-long dynamic personal development program. They *know* that to build a business, **they must build themself. To help others, they must first help themselves;** and **to change the world, we must change ourselves!**
• let opportunity drift away.	♦ **realize opportunity is knocking. Seize** the **opportunity** while it is still an opportunity.
• miss the point unless it's hammered home hard, directly and way too bluntly.	♦ **have the experience** to "listen between the lines" and intuit.
• love to *receive* recognition.	♦ love to **give recognition.**
• step on people to get ahead. They celebrate and gloat over lucky breaks which create apparent achievement.	♦ **recognize emerging leaders and value their contribution** to the organization.
• struggle being leaders.	♦ see *True Leadership* as a **way of life.**

Cubic Zirconia "Leaders" Usually:	True Diamond Leaders:
• focus on the worst in people.	♦ are **happy, smart, successful, clever, sharp, sometimes cool, overall have an attitude of gratitude spirit** and are **joyful!**
• know it all. Always say "I know, I know . . ."	♦ are **always students.**
• settle for less.	♦ **achieve greatness.** Choose to **go for it** *for as long as it takes*—have stickability.
• wonder what others can do for them.	♦ **make a difference in people's lives.** Help others exceed even their own expectations. **Believe in you** before you believe in yourself.
• fulfill a personal, selfish ambition to shortcut the process and gain admiration.	♦ **empower** as many people as possible to become the very best they can be.
• reduce the leader's power which only reflects on their insecurity.	♦ know that their **leadership just gets stronger when attacked.**
• try to influence others to support their selfish, controlling views. They resist taking a stand for change.	♦ **take a stand** because of their wisdom and experience. They understand that nothing is going to stay the same forever and **embrace positive change.**
• unplug from the main source of inspiration, motivation and education.	♦ stay **"plugged in" to the True Leader** because they know that the *True Leader* has the experience and wisdom they can learn from.

Cubic Zirconia "Leaders" Usually:	True Diamond Leaders:
• use best intentions and the weak phrase: "I'll try . . ."	♦ **accept reality.** They **seek to find solutions** to challenges worth solving and *elect* which battles to win and which to *lose*. They understand that best intentions have no value without results. They follow Yoda's admonition: **"There is no try, there is only do."**

Cubic Zirconia "Leaders" Make:	True Diamond Leaders:
• a big deal if they have to sacrifice.	♦ **make sacrifices quietly.** Know that there are temporary sacrifices on the path to obtaining their dreams, but the *rewards are permanent.*
• excuses. Are part of the challenge.	♦ don't make excuses. **Create results instead!** Are part of the solution.
• mistakes and justify them.	♦ **make mistakes,** and correct them and go on.

Cubic Zirconia "Leaders" Think They Are:	True Diamond Leaders:
• always perfect and correct.	♦ **know** they're not perfect.
• perfect.	♦ are **accountable**—have some humility.
• do busy work and wonder where their day went.	♦ **work**—productively—every way, every day.

Cubic Zirconia "Leaders" Rarely:	True Diamond Leaders:
• if ever, review progress.	♦ **review progress** constantly.
• perform alone—must be cheered for. They crave personal recognition and want to be the hero.	♦ **perform alone,** even when no one is there to cheer. The real true Network Marketing Champions *build leaders and make them successful.*
• welcome change. They can't handle the pain and stress of change.	♦ **initiate change** to improve the quality of their organization. Have the *courage to take action,* however personally painful the solution may be.

Cubic Zirconia "Leaders" Seek:	True Diamond Leaders:
• admiration through self-promotion. They want to train and teach long before they have a worthy message that gets results.	♦ don't **seek admiration,** but naturally receive it through *attraction.*
• to be in front of the room teaching and training but will not have production numbers to have earned that right.	♦ **want to help others** be in front of the room who have achieved strong current production numbers and have earned the right.

Cubic Zirconia "Leaders" See:	True Diamond Leaders:
• all changes as problems. They're usually misinformed.	♦ **concentrate** on preventing challenges—they get the facts, use intuition and insight and explore the possibilities.
• difficulty and challenges as their enemy, not their stepping stones.	♦ **see** obstacles as something to stand *on* so that they can see the goal more clearly.
• themselves as peers or better than their leader. Are disrespectful.	♦ are **respectful** to those who have taught them well. **They build valuable relationships** and **strive to get along,** because they know that is the best strategy for their business.

Cubic Zirconia "Leaders" Think They Have:	True Diamond Leaders:
• reached the top long, long before they actually have.	♦ are always getting better at **listening, learning, conducting meetings** and **teaching others.**
• to "win" every single battle.	♦ *select* **which battles to win** and which they can easily afford to *lose*.
• to watch TV news and read the newspaper "cover to cover."	♦ **feed their minds** by **reading** books, **listening** to self-improvement tapes, turning their cars into classrooms, watch business-related videos, listen to Freedom Radio while *doing* something *productive* for family or business.

Cubic Zirconia "Leaders" Want:	True Diamond Leaders
• everyone to love them.	♦ **know** they can't please everyone—*and some just aren't even worth trying to please. Oh well.*
• to be pushy.	♦ **know** they must **push people out of their comfort zones** to empower them to success.
• to waste a ton of time trying to prove their point.	♦ don't **waste time** on people or things that won't matter anyway.

Cubic Zirconia "Leaders" Whine:	True Diamond Leaders:
• "if . . ." or "if only . . ."	♦ **state** when.
• about their "addiction" to diet colas or other unhealthy things.	♦ **treat** their bodies with great respect and strive to take the best care of themselves.
• "I've tried for years and am not making any money." Don't realize that if the effort is really there, the results come.	♦ **never expect** results without effort. They know that if they ardently desire and are willing to work towards a goal, it must ultimately come to pass.
• about what they are going to accomplish (they're always "a-fixin' to do it").	♦ **quietly** get the job done and achieve goals, then set new ones.

Chapter 7

True Leaders Listen

I think the one lesson I have learned is that there is no substitute for paying attention.

~ Diane Sawyer

The most basic of all human needs is the need to understand and be understood.

~ Ralph Nichols

We do not believe in ourselves until someone reveals that deep inside us is something valuable, worth listening to, worthy of our trust, sacred to our touch. Once we believe in ourselves we can risk curiosity, wonder, spontaneous delight or any experience that reveals the human spirit.

~ e.e. cummings

Children have never been very good at listening to their elders, but they have never failed to imitate them.

~ James Baldwin

You cannot truly listen to anyone and do anything else at the same time.

~ M. Scott Peck

If speaking is silver, then listening is gold.

~ Turkish Proverb

Easy listening exists only on the radio.
~ **David Barkan**

Instead of listening to what is being said to them, many managers are already listening to what they are going to say.
~ **Anonymous**

Careful the things you say, children will listen. Careful the things you do, children will see. And learn. Children may not obey, but children will listen. Children will look to you for which way to turn, to learn what to be. Careful before you say, 'Listen to me.' Children will listen.
~ **Witch** in *Into the Woods* **(1990) (TV)**

The principle of listening, someone has said, is to develop a big ear rather than a big mouth.
~ **Howard G. and Jeanne Hendricks**

Now a man cannot listen to another while he will have all the talk and discourse to himself.
~ **C.H. Spurgeon**

Freedom is when the people can speak, democracy is when the government listens.
~ **Alastair Farrugia**

The best way to persuade people is with your ears—by listening to them.
~ **Dean Rusk**

It is the disease of not listening, the malady of not marking, that I am troubled with.
~ **Shakespeare**

The way to stay fresh is you never stop traveling, you never stop listening. You never stop asking people what they think.
~ **Rene McPherson, former chairman, Dana**

Listening is an attitude of the heart, a genuine desire to be with another which both attracts and heals.
~ **J. Isham**

The key to success is to get out into the store and listen to what the associates have to say. It's terribly important for everyone to get involved. Our best ideas come from clerks and stock boys.
~ **Sam Walton**

The jungle speaks to me because I know how to listen.
~ **Mowgli in** *The Jungle Book* **(1994)**

It is difficult for anyone to speak when you listen only to yourself.
~ **Lorna Bounty in The Man with a Cloak (1951)**

It is the province of knowledge to speak. And it is the privilege of wisdom to listen.
~ **Oliver Wendell Holmes**

If the person you are talking to doesn't appear to be listening, be patient. It may simply be that he has a small piece of fluff in his ear.
~ *Pooh's Little Instruction Book,*
inspired by A. A. Milne

Listening is a magnetic and strange thing, a creative force. The friends who listen to us are the ones we move toward. When we are listened to, it creates us, makes us unfold and expand.
~ **Karl Menninger**

So, when you are listening to somebody, completely, attentively, then you are listening not only to the words, but also to the feeling of what is being conveyed, to the whole of it, not part of it.
~ Jiddu Krishnamurti

A good listener tries to understand what the other person is saying. In the end he may disagree sharply, but because he disagrees, he wants to know exactly what it is he is disagreeing with.
~ Kenneth A. Wells

Opportunities are often missed because we are broadcasting when we should be listening.
~ Author Unknown

The time to stop talking is when the other person nods his head affirmatively but says nothing.
~ Author Unknown

Listening, not imitation, may be the sincerest form of flattery.
~ Dr. Joyce Brothers

Chapter 8

Leadership Tips from True Leaders

You can buy a person's time; you can buy a person's physical presence at a given place; you can even buy a measured number of a person's skilled muscular motions per hour. But you can not buy genuine enthusiasm . . . you can *not* buy loyalty . . you can not buy leadership or the devotion of hearts, minds, or soul. *These you must earn.*
~ Jan Ruhe and Art Burleigh

Sometimes if you want to see a change for the better, you have to take things into your own hands. Once you decide to be at the level of choice, you take responsibility for your life and gain control of it. If *you* don't run your own life, someone *else* will. You are in control of your life to the degree that *you* make the decisions. If you let others make decisions for you, you have no control. *When you control the decisions, you control the actions.* So, take charge of your life. You do not have to ask permission of other people. Don't give someone veto power over your life. If not you, then who? If not now, then when?
~ Jan Ruhe and Art Burleigh

I didn't have a lot of organizational ability, nor insight into the challenges of the new nation. I did have the ability to deal effectively with diverse personalities.

Know this, many of the founding fathers of the United States of America were extremely difficult men. Genius has a habit of producing complex personalities. I was able to work with the most complicated people, accepting both their faults and their failings as natural. I was once asked how I could possibly tolerate Thomas Jefferson, that "overbearing, intolerant, impatient, aristocratic" individual. I explained that Jefferson's *personality was his wife's challenge*. I only dealt with the man's genius.

~ George Washington

Nothing in this world can take the place of *persistence*. Talent will not; nothing is more common than unsuccessful men with talent. Genius will not; unrewarded genius is almost a proverb. Education will not; the world is full of educated derelicts. *Persistence and determination* alone are omnipotent. The slogan "press on" has solved and always will solve the problems of the human race.

~ Calvin Coolidge

You can demonstrate the art of leadership with a simple piece of string. Put the string on a table. *Pull it*, and it will follow where you wish. *Push it*, and it will go nowhere at all. It's just that way when it comes to leading people.

~ General Eisenhower

I would rather make mistakes in kindness and compassion than work miracles in unkindness and hardness.

~ Mother Teresa

When you are making a success of something, it's not work. It's a way of life. You enjoy yourself because you are making your contribution to the world.
~ **Former race car driver and STP king,**
Andy Granatelli

Get someone else to blow your horn and the sound will carry twice as far.
~ **Will Rogers**

It is one of the most beautiful compensations of this life that no person can sincerely try to help another without helping himself.
~ **Ralph Waldo Emerson**

The way I see it, if you want the rainbow, you gotta put up with the rain.
~ **Dolly Parton**

It is not the critic who counts, not the man who points out how the strong man stumbled or where the doer of deeds could have done better. The credit belongs to the man who is actually *in the arena*; whose face is marred by dust and sweat and blood; who strives valiantly; who errs and comes short again and again; who knows the great enthusiasms, the great devotions and spends himself in a worthy cause; who, at the best, knows in the end the triumph of high achievement; and who, at the worst, if he fails, at least fails while daring greatly, so that his place shall never be with those cold and timid souls who know *neither* victory nor defeat.
~ **Theodore Roosevelt**

Don't listen to those who say, *"It's not done that way."* Maybe it's not, but maybe you'll do it anyway. Don't listen to those who say, *"You're taking too big a chance."* Michelangelo would have painted the Sistine Chapel's *floor*, and it would surely be rubbed out by today. Most important, don't listen when the little voice of fear inside you rears its ugly head and says, *"They're all smarter than you out there. They're more talented, they're taller, blonder, prettier, luckier and they have connections. They have a cousin who took out Meryl Streep's baby-sitter . . ."* I firmly believe that if you follow a path that interests you, not to the exclusion of love, sensitivity, and cooperation with others, but with the **strength of conviction,** that you can move others by your own efforts, and do not make success or failure the criteria by which you live, the chances are you'll be a person worthy of your own respect.

~ **Neil Simon, Playwright**

It's not so much how busy you are, but why you are busy. The bee is praised. The mosquito is swatted.

~ **Marie O'Connor**

Leadership is not magnetic personality—that can just as well be a glib tongue. It is not "making friends and influencing people"- that is flattery. *Leadership is lifting a person's vision to higher sights, raising a person's performance to a higher standard, building a personality beyond its normal limitations.*

~ **Peter Drucker**

Watch your thoughts; they become words. Watch your words; they become actions. Watch your actions; they become habits. Watch your habits; they become character. Watch your character; it becomes your destiny.
~ **Frank Outlaw**

Hate is like acid. It can damage the vessel in which it is stored as well as destroy the object on which it is poured.
~ **Ann Landers**

Consider how hard it is to change yourself and you will understand what little chance you have of trying to change others.
~**Jacob Braude**

I'm just a plow hand from Arkansas, but I have learned how to hold a team together. How to lift some men up, how to calm down others, until finally they've got one heartbeat together, the team. There are just three things I'd ever say:
If anything goes bad, *I did it.*
If anything goes semi-good, then *we did it.*
If anything goes real good, then *you did it.*
That's all it takes to get people to win
football games for you.
~ **Coach Bear Bryant,
University of Alabama**

Chapter 9

Inspiring Little Gems

- After actor/director Michael Douglas had been in five blockbuster films, his father, actor Kirk Douglas, wrote him a note. It said: "Michael, I am more proud of *how* you handle success than I am of your success." It's a note Michael Douglas treasures.

- Consider the hammer—it keeps pounding away. It makes mistakes, and when it does, it starts all over. It uses its head. It's one of the few knockers in the world that does anything constructive. It doesn't fly off the handle. It finds the point and drives it home.

- Gregory Peck and a friend once walked into a crowded restaurant and had to stand with others waiting for a table. "Tell them *who you are*," urged the friend. "If you have to tell them *who* you are, you aren't anybody," replied Peck.

- If you are feeling low, don't despair. The sun has a sinking spell every night, but it comes back up every morning!

- It is said, courtesy is contagious. Let's have an epidemic!

- Kites rise against the wind, not with it.

- Learn for the mistakes of others—you can never live long enough to make them all yourself.

- Setbacks pave the way for comebacks.

- The perseverance of the Colorado River made the Grand Canyon. The perseverance of Thomas Edison gave us the electric light. The perseverance of Abraham Lincoln won him the presidency, abolished slavery and preserved the Union of the United States!

- The pessimist complains about the wind; the optimist expects it to change; the realist adjusts the sails.

- The Spirit of the Hive at work—Bees show us something about teamwork and leadership. On warm days about half the bees in a hive stay inside beating their wings while the other half go out to gather pollen and nectar. Because of the beating wings, the temperature inside the hive is about 10 degrees cooler than outside. The bees rotate duties, and the cooling bees on one day are honey gatherers the next day.

Let's Lead

People don't want to be managed.

They want to be led.

Whoever heard of a world manager?

World leader, yes.

Educational leader.

Political Leader.

Religious leader.

Scout leader.

Community leader.

Labor leader.

Business leader.

They lead.

They don't manage.

The carrot always wins over the stick.

Ask your horse.

You can lead your horse to water,

but you can't manage him to drink.

If you want to manage somebody, manage yourself.

Do that well and you'll be ready to stop managing.

And start leading.

~ Contributed by Richard Brooke

The Leadership Pledge
I Will Lead!

The Die has been cast, I've stepped over the Line.
The Decision has been done, the Destiny determined.
I will no longer Vacillate, I will no longer Vacate.
I will no longer Listen to, Listen at,
or Listen in on Losing . . .

I will not be Defeated, Dejected, Diluted, or Detoured.
I will no longer Navigate with the Needle of
Negativity.

The Direction's been Decided, the Trail to be Tried.
The Destiny's directed, the Future Forged.

I will not be Pulled on, Pulled In, Pulled down, or
Pulled Out.
I won't Back Up, Back Down, Back Away, or Back Off.
I won't Give in, Give out, or Give way to Defeat.
I will no longer Meander in the Maze of Mediocrity.

I will no longer Conform to the Cancer of Can't.
I now will Confirm the Condition of Can.

I will Probe the Possibilities, Pick the Probabilities.
I will Focus on the Fire, and Heat it even hotter.

I will never Give up, Let up, Set up, or Shut up on
Success.

I am reaching for the Ring, and Pulling on the Power.
I've quit Wishing, Hoping, Wasting, and Whining.
I now will aggressively gear into the Word GO.

And I am Determined to Dare to Do till I Drop.
I will withstand the Whining Winds of Defeat.

And I will be Powerfully Persistent,
Consistent, and Insistent,
 to get out of Life What I truly deserve.

Because I am Willing, I am Waiting, I am Worthy,
and understand the Only Defeat is From Within.

I now know that beyond any Shadow of the Cloud of
Doubt,
There is No Shadow, There is no Cloud, And There is
No Doubt . . .

I WILL LEAD!

~ Doug Firebaugh

Doug Firebaugh is Chairman/CEO of PassionFire International. He is a trainer, author and international speaker. He was full time in MLM for 10 years and built an international business. Doug has a talk radio show called "Maximum Fire" focused on Self-Growth and Leadership, and over 20,000 people read his weekly PassionFire e-zines. He lives in Kentucky.

doug@talking.cc
www.mlmleadership.com

Chapter 10

The Jan Ruhe/Art Burleigh
Leadership Study

Here is a master checklist of every *QUALITY* of a *True Leader* that we could collect. We are sure there are more! There are over 250 qualities that we have discovered. Just go down this checklist and check off what you have already mastered, then you can go back and work on those areas that you might want to develop further. Good luck! This is just a starting place!

True Leaders act:

❏ **courageously.**

❏ with **conviction** and **enthusiasm.**

❏ *as if* **it was impossible to fail.**

True Leaders are:

❏ **able to pay back** what they have been blessed with, and create—for both themselves *and* for an emerging group of leaders on their team—a secure, happy and prosperous life of purpose.

❏ **able to say they are sorry** even when they are not at fault—they don't fret about who is right or wrong.

❏ **accessible.**

❏ **approachable.**

❏ **aware** of emerging leaders, to **mentor,** and **build** into stronger leaders.

❏ **balanced.**

❏ **built,** not born.

- ❑ **careful** how they turn down ideas that can't be used.
- ❑ **cautious** of grandiosity, the belief that they already **have** all the answers.
- ❑ **charitable** to others.
- ❑ **coachable.**
- ❑ **driven** by *big* visions and strong self-motivation.
- ❑ **eager** to go and do!
- ❑ **eager** to learn new, more efficient ways to prospect, sponsor, retail, and lead.
- ❑ easy to **talk to.**
- ❑ **enthusiastic.**
- ❑ **excited.**
- ❑ **fair.**
- ❑ **experts** in internal geography.
- ❑ first a **loyal follower.**
- ❑ **great** at giving **encouragement.**
- ❑ **great listeners.**
- ❑ **honest.**
- ❑ **hope coaches.**
- ❑ **interested.**
- ❑ **kind.**
- ❑ **loyal.** The key to loyalty is deserving it, and showing that you do.
- ❑ **modest.**
- ❑ so busy **giving** recognition that they don't need it.
- ❑ **not disagreeable.**
- ❑ **on time.**
- ❑ **open-minded.**
- ❑ **polite.**
- ❑ presently **professional students** of the business.
- ❑ **responsible.**

❑ **sensitive** to the feelings, emotions and experiences of other people.

❑ sincerely and **genuinely interested** in the present and future of those who work with them.

❑ **tolerant.**

❑ **willing** to **listen.**

❑ **willing** to **travel.**

❑ **ready** to take on the role of a *True Leader.*

True Leaders always:

❑ **build** and **test** both courage and stamina throughout their team.

❑ **give credit** to those who help them succeed.

❑ **look** at the next rung on the ladder of the compensation plan.

❑ **return** phone calls, no matter how difficult the conversation will be.

❑ **set** new, higher **goals**—for themselves and for their organization.

❑ use the **Golden Rule:** "Do unto others, as you would have them do unto you."

True leaders appreciate:

❑ and **understand** the **feelings** of other people.

❑ **others' viewpoints,** challenges, hopes and ambitions.

True Leaders ask for:

❑ **suggestions** about challenges.

❑ **understanding** and **tolerance.**

True Leaders believe:

❑ in the **dignity of labor,** that the world owes no person a living, but that it owes every person an *opportunity* to make a living.

❑ in the **sacredness of a promise,** that a person's word should be as good as their bond.

❑ **in themselves.**

❑ that **love** can overcome hate.

True Leaders depend on:
- ❑ **followers.** If people don't follow your lead voluntarily, if they always have to be forced, then that is not *True Leadership*.
- ❑ **their ability** to make people want to follow—voluntarily.

True Leaders don't:
- ❑ **brag openly** about business successes or their percentage of growth. They prefer to smile all the way to the bank!
- ❑ **discourage** their people.
- ❑ **just happen.**
- ❑ just **show up** one day.
- ❑ **let a few challenges poison** their outlook.
- ❑ **make major decisions on minor matters.** They save their real effort for big and important decisions.
- ❑ **play** the blame game.
- ❑ **straddle** the fence.
- ❑ **strive** to do everything themselves.
- ❑ **tolerate** destructive relationships indefinitely. They **take action.**
- ❑ **turn down** people's ideas **abruptly.**

True Leaders empower others:
- ❑ into stronger **leadership** roles.
- ❑ with the **vitality** of their beliefs.

True Leaders get:
- ❑ **all the facts** when they are told only one side. They make up their mind, then issue their decision with complete confidence.
- ❑ **good suggestions** from their people.
- ❑ **knowledge** from many sources.
- ❑ lots of **great kicks** out of life.
- ❑ **recharged.**
- ❑ up early in the morning ready to take on the day.

True Leaders give:
- ❑ and **share credit** liberally.
- ❑ high **effort.**
- ❑ intelligent effort.
- ❑ **loyalty.**
- ❑ **themselves deadlines** for making decisions.

True Leaders have:
- ❑ a sense of **urgency.**
- ❑ **allies**—so they can **network** with like-minded colleagues.
- ❑ an essential **obligation** to live their lives according to the principles they espouse. People are hungry for good strong leadership. They're watching what you *do*.
- ❑ **confidence.**
- ❑ **ethics.**
- ❑ **goals**—written, posted and in clear view.
- ❑ **courage.**
- ❑ **creativity.**
- ❑ **faith.**
- ❑ **feelings.**
- ❑ **goals** and **vision** that are clear and strong—so they can succeed faster.
- ❑ greater time **freedom,** financial freedom, freedom from the rat race, a chance to finally move from money to meaning, from receiving to contribution.
- ❑ **high morals.**
- ❑ **imagination.**
- ❑ **integrity.**
- ❑ **personal growth** and **development** programs for their everyday life.
- ❑ **time** for their families.
- ❑ **time** to receive important calls and to pay worthwhile visits.

True Leaders know:
- ❑ it all starts with the **fire of desire!**
- ❑ *no* **pain,** *no* **gain.**
- ❑ there is a lot to **learn.**
- ❑ **what** they stand for.
- ❑ **what** they won't stand for.
- ❑ **where they stand** and what else **they need to do** to accomplish their goals!

True Leaders know how to:
- ❑ **bless** and **release** with ease.
- ❑ **move on** when they make proposals that are well thought out that are rejected by middle-management mentality.
- ❑ **pay attention to other True Leaders** who overcame challenges, so they don't have to endure all those painful experiences first hand themselves, and their journey to success can be accelerated.
- ❑ **teach** and **train**—to provide **high quality mentoring.**

True Leaders know that:
- ❑ **character,** not wealth or power or position, is of supreme worth.
- ❑ **leading takes just good old-fashioned guts.**
- ❑ **respect** isn't something that comes automatically just because you have people working with you.
- ❑ their job is to **build** *more* leaders.
- ❑ they **can't please everyone.**
- ❑ they **get** the **best efforts** out of people by working *with* them, by helping them to do their best, by showing them how to be more **productive.** Most people want to do a good job, as long as someone **appreciates** their efforts and **encourages** them. That's where *True Leaders* put their greatest effort, to **show people** that their work is **valuable** and **appreciated.**
- ❑ the qualities of excellent leadership today are the same

as those of heroes and sheros dating back to ancient mythology!

❑ their **small gestures** send big messages.

True Leaders know the:

❑ **information, by studying it** well enough to be able to teach it to others.

❑ *pathway* is already well worn by all the heroes who have gone before them.

❑ **Real Deal**, they are **authentic.**

True Leaders learn:

❑ from other *True Leaders* through tapes, books, and online.

❑ how to **empower** others.

❑ how to **communicate** correctly.

❑ **to know** when things are right and when they're finally on a faster track to success.

❑ **to be positive** in all their actions. They don't delay or sit on the fence. Indecision is a decision; so they don't hang out in indecision.

True Leaders listen to:

❑ hours of tapes.

❑ people who are actually **living the lifestyle** they want.

True Leaders look:

❑ at all events that happen as opportunities to **personally grow.**

❑ for leaders with whom to **build** fine, new, long-term relationships.

True Leaders are never:

❑ **surprised** by what others call unexpected connections.

❑ content to **put off** until tomorrow what they can get done today.

❑ **satisfied** with the status quo.

True Leaders realize:
- ❑ it's a **tough journey** with plenty of **challenges** and **learning experiences.**

True Leaders realize that:
- ❑ **good relations** between people are conducive to good work.

- ❑ if two people are hopelessly abrasive to each other, they should consider **reorganizing** in a manner that will keep them out of each other's way.

- ❑ it's **smart** to have days that consist of leaving about four to five things unsaid.

- ❑ they have to sometimes **make tough decisions** that they wish they did not have to make.

True Leaders show:
- ❑ **compassion** for those who they love and appreciate.

- ❑ **consideration** for the feelings of others.

- ❑ **interest** in others.

True Leaders show people:
- ❑ **courtesy** by taking their suggestions under advisement.

- ❑ the **systems** and **tools** that work.

- ❑ how coming into partnership with them and what they have to offer **can benefit** that prospect by helping *them* get what *they* want.

True Leaders take:
- ❑ a **friendly, pleasant approach.**

- ❑ a genuine **interest** in what others say.

- ❑ **an interest** in all of their people.

- ❑ **care** of their body.

- ❑ **initiative** to seek those more talented than they are to build relationships with.

- ❑ **massive action.**

- ❑ **time** for themselves.

- ❑ **time to think.**

True Leaders try:
- ❑ to **communicate** until they find the cause of an upset.
- ❑ to **eliminate** head-to-head competition.
- ❑ **fail, learn, adjust/correct/re-aim** and **try again.**

True Leaders understand:
- ❑ people, **how they feel** and the best way to **influence** them.
- ❑ now and then, people rub each other the wrong way, so they **look for a constructive solution to eliminate irritation, relieve tension,** and **restore cooperation.** If people don't want to cooperate, the *True Leader* understands and blesses and releases.

True Leaders understand that:
- ❑ there are **reasons** why people succeed and only **excuses** why they don't.
- ❑ there is a **solution** to any challenge.

True Leaders:
- ❑ **achieve success** and keep moving up!
- ❑ **always keep the following in mind** when making decisions: What will happen if I do *this?* What will happen if I do *that?*
- ❑ **analyze decisions** made by others. If they don't agree, they determine if their reasons for disagreement are sound and logical. They don't let someone try to "reason" with them when they *know* that they're *right!*
- ❑ are **not perfect**—they know they are human.
- ❑ **are their own Public Relations agents.** They do everything they can to make their name known. If they intend to be a heavy hitter, they know they need to become well known. People must recognize their name immediately. To do this, they get their name in the paper and online whenever possible. They offer to speak to church or civic groups without any sort of reimbursement as long as the group promises to send out notices on e-mail loops and put an ad in the local paper publicizing the event.

❑ **aren't** always "in charge" or "in control"—but they are aware, alert, in touch and out in front.

❑ **aren't surprised** by miracles, they expect them.

❑ **attend** the right events. Just attending an event is not going to make any difference unless it can improve your bottom line.

❑ **avoid** killing all ideas of others.

❑ believe that **right** can and will triumph over might.

❑ **blaze** a trail and **attain** success, stature and respect in many fields.

❑ **build** their own library.

❑ **build** new leaders and make *them* successful.

❑ **can not take** a pill that will instantly make them a leader.

❑ **can take** a stand.

❑ **change.**

❑ **deal** with others openly, honestly and fairly.

❑ **delegate tasks**—both high and low priority.

❑ **delegate responsibility.**

❑ **desire to provide** a better and brighter future for those they honor and love.

❑ **develop people.**

❑ **develop relationships** and friendships with other *True Leaders*, serve them, help them—and receive rewards by gaining knowledge and skills they lacked.

❑ **direct** people to the resources they need to build their own belief systems.

❑ **discover** talents and abilities in people that they didn't know they had.

❑ **discuss** their ideas occasionally with others.

❑ **do** things beyond the "normal" range of achievement.

❑ **guard secrets** of their successline or poor behavior like they would their daughter's morals. Coca-Cola and

Kentucky Fried Chicken are fine examples of keeping secret recipes for decades.

❏ **educate** themselves, then bring back the new ideas.

❏ **embrace** positive change.

❏ **encourage** people.

❏ **engage** in the process of *transformation*—from unknowing **to knowing.**

❏ **facilitate** new relationships.

❏ **feed their mind.** Books, seminars and tapes are brain food.

❏ **find** and **access** many highly intelligent, gifted and inspiring mentors.

❏ **first understand** by asking questions and listening.

❏ **follow the Golden Rule:** "Do unto others as you would have them do unto you."

❏ **follow** *True Leaders*. It's not a cult to be a follower of a *True Leader* if that *True Leader* has integrity to always be looking out for what is best for the entire organization.

❏ **forget** other's **mistakes.**

❏ **go** to where other *True Leaders* are teaching to attend their seminars, *no matter what the investment.*

❏ **go** to work on their personal growth and development programs, for *years.*

❏ **guide** people, just as heroes and sheros were guided in ancient times.

❏ **have the courage to act,** to do what has to be done, despite the costs, the hardships, the hazards, the critics and the sacrifices. **People follow courage!**

❏ **help** others succeed.

❏ **initiate** positive change.

❏ **develop relationships** with those whom they admire the most.

❏ **empower** their team.

❑ **know** that they are not responsible for what *others* think of them. They are only responsible for what they think of *themselves.*

❑ **lead** by example.

❑ **know** that you can go clear up to the very top.

❑ **lead** people who might not normally interact with each other into productive conversations.

❑ **lead people by emotions** more than by logic and reason.

❑ **learn** from the mistakes of others.

❑ **listen.**

❑ **make** mistakes and try to learn from them.

❑ **mentor** people into stronger leadership roles.

❑ **navigate** along the way. While those 'bumps along the road' can be frustrating, they ultimately provide great depth of character and conviction in our beliefs.

❑ **need** a *healthy* ego, *and they know* that a *big ego* that's out of control can kill them and make them look absolutely foolish.

❑ **network** with other leaders.

❑ **network.**

❑ **organize.**

❑ **paint** vivid mental pictures for others.

❑ **pave** the way and get massive results.

❑ **perform** responsibly.

❑ personally **grow.**

❑ **point out** that people's value depends on their ability to get along with others.

❑ **praise** others.

❑ **protect** their team from danger, while doing their best to open their eyes to reality.

❑ **provide** direction.

❑ **put** themselves in others' shoes and **consider** what their reaction will be to things.

❑ are **qualified to lead** because of their **learned expertise.**

❑ **rarely** become overexcited or fly off the handle.

❑ **read.** They know that readers are leaders.

❑ **read** hundreds of books.

❑ **reject suggestions gently,** giving reasons and admitting that they could be wrong.

❑ remain **attentive,** aware and focused as they strive to "get it" along their journey.

❑ **remain** students always.

❑ **run their own** incentive programs. They don't wait for their company to do it.

❑ **show people how** to make a fantastic future *real* for those who sincerely want that and are willing to work hard to achieve it!

❑ **require** a journey. The sooner they depart, the faster they will get to their destination.

❑ **require faith** that their associates will always try to do their best.

❑ **respect** those who have helped them succeed.

❑ **see** new patterns and possibilities that allow for important innovations or realizations.

❑ **seek** first to understand, *then* to be understood.

❑ **sense** when the right *questions* need to be asked to find *solutions* to challenges.

❑ **smile.**

❑ **spot** subtle **relationships** that can be valuable.

❑ stop occasionally to **ask** people **questions** about their work.

❑ stress that **cooperation** is essential for the good of everyone.

❑ are **strong** enough to take a stand on values and principles.

❑ **supervise.**

❑ **take action.**

❑ **tell** people over and over that they believe in them.

❑ **thank** others for their interest and ideas.

❑ **train.**

❑ **transfer** their vision to others and become the **substance** of their **hope,** their dream for new success by coming into **partnership** with them and their team.

❑ **trust** others.

❑ **use** resources like *Upline®* magazine, *Network Marketing Lifestyles Magazine*, MLM University, Jan Ruhe's Book-of-the-Month Club, Freedom Radio, and a host of great web sites, including www.janruhe. com, www.artburleigh.com and www.mlm-metro.com.

❑ **vary their routine.**

❑ **walk** the **talk** and earn the **respect** and **trust** of their colleagues.

❑ **walk** the **walk,** *and* talk the talk.

❑ **work** hard.

❑ **work** with two to three emerging leaders.

❑ **zero in** on small things people do right.

We have a premonition
that soars on Silver Wings.
We dream of your accomplishments
and other wondrous things.
We do not know beneath what sky
that you will conquer fate.
We only know it will be high and
We only know you will all be great!

Art Burleigh and Jan Ruhe

Chapter 11

You Are On the Right Path

CONGRATULATIONS! YOU ARE THE PROUD OWNER OF this fantastic book! We believe that it is one of the *finest books* on leadership today. It represents the culmination of many hundreds of hours of research in our Burleigh & Ruhe Leadership Institute, as well as many interviews with big thinkers, in-the-trenches leaders, and men and women from all companies and all walks of life who have made themselves *True Leaders.*

Suppose you were given a plot of beautiful mountain land, and told you could do whatever you wished with it, *provided that* **you** performed all the work *yourself.* You walk around your new property, taking in the vast, panoramic view of the spectacular valley far below and the majestic peaks in the distance. The invigorating air is crystal clear. There's no haze anywhere, and the aroma of the pristine pine forest is intoxicating as it sweeps around you and the huge, grassy clearing where you proudly stand. Eagles soar over the nearby cliffs—silently swooping up on thermals with their immense seven-foot wingspans. *What* a stunning and inspiring place! What will *you do* with this incredible opportunity?

After evaluating this phenomenal new property and what's been handed to you, you decide to build a fabulous cabin with huge, high windows, beautiful, thick, sturdy logs and colorful river-rock walls. Would you then proceed to merely scratch an outline in the dirt, invest in a few basic tools, scrounge around for scrap materials and construct the retreat of your dreams from your makeshift plan and meager preparations?

Of course not! No sane person, who truly appreciated and understood this opportunity of a lifetime to create "the retreat of their dreams," would begin to build without a thorough assessment of the available materials, tools, and most important, without a definite *plan!*

Yet, day after day, people stumble forward with this same kind of inadequate approach to their lives *and* to their business. An unusually large percentage of people around the world think about, talk about, and attempt to build bright futures without *any* direction, organization, leadership or definite plans. How tragic!

You now know that what you hold in your hands is a treasury of information and tips on *True Leadership* by *True Leaders* that can *guide you* and *help you* with your blueprint for your successful future. You have now had a glimpse of how these leaders work, what they do, what's important to them, how they think, how they influence others and who *they* consider to be *True Leaders*. This collection of wisdom can help *you* become the *True Leader* you are meant to be, and it can also help countless people on your team!

While writing, we thought of all the leaders who had inspired us in our personal growth and development. We felt it would be great to include some of these Masters in this book so that you could benefit from their thoughts. These aren't all of the *True Leaders* who ever inspired us, yet this sure is a fabulous collection of great ideas by exceptional people. We hope that you found some clear answers on what to work on as you progress along *your* path to becoming a *True Leader.*

Many of our leader friends happily agreed to contribute their wisdom. It's with a gratitude attitude that we thank all of these contributors. Through challenges, all of these Masters have navigated to success and generously share their wisdom.

Each of these Masters could have had over a page to list their accomplishments. We encourage you to get their books and tapes. To have been invited to contribute to this book we wanted the cream of the crop of Masters. Within minutes of being invited to write "their take" on *True Leadership,* every one of these Masters had their articles to us. They weren't too busy. They did not make excuses; they stopped and made this treasury of *True Leadership* tips happen.

It's just like a choir, we all need to hear from lots of different voices to become the great masterpiece that we all are. And, you will find that we are all a lot more alike than we are different.

Clearly you are on the right path. We hope that you have found one or more of these articles and chapters that will help you embrace the fact that **you** can *be* a *True Leader.* It all starts with the fire of desire!

We believe in you and look forward to our paths crossing while we all enjoy the wonders of this planet Earth. Be the best you can be, push yourself, always be the student, feed your mind, ponder the wisdom shared in this book and then go for greatness!

Good Luck! This book is to help you become a *True Leader* of the future. *True Leaders* are made, not born. So why not make yourself a *True Leader?*

Our last word?

Being a True Leader

is not about making

yourself more powerful.

It's about making

the people around you more powerful!

Best wishes out there in Leadershipping land,

Art Burleigh and Jan Ruhe

About the Authors

Together, we have 33 years of experience in Network Marketing and more than 100 years of living on this magnificent planet. We have mastered every part of the Network Marketing business.

Jan Ruhe

- is a mother of three children—Sarah, Clayton and Ashley White.
- is an *Upline*® Master, and a contributing writer for the *Upline*® Journal.
- has been in Network Marketing for over 20 years, since 1980.
- is the top Diamond distributor for her company.
- is a world class international Network Marketing/Sales Trainer/ Speaker.
- has trained over 50,000 people worldwide.
- is the author of *MLM Nuts $ Bolts* and *Fire Up!* and the creator of the *Fire Up!* music CD.
- has well over $100 Million total organizational sales in her career.
- holds the record for promoting the most leaders in her company for the decade of the 90s.
- is in the Network Marketing Hall of Fame.
- has a B.A. in Sociology from Texas Tech University.
- has been quoted and written about in many books and appeared in dozens of magazines.
- is a daily speaker on Freedom Radio, worldwide web.

- lives with her husband, Bill, in Colorado.
- received the 1998 Woman of Distinction award in the International Network Marketing Directory.
- became a Millionaire through Network Marketing.

www.janruhe.com
1-970-927-3010

Art Burleigh

- has been in Network Marketing since 1987.
- is a top Double Diamond Executive distributor for his company and received their 1999 Leadership Award.
- serves on the Executive Council for Essentially Yours Industries.
- in the last four years of the 1990s, his Network Marketing organization sold over $92 Million in products.
- is a contributing writer for the *Upline®* Journal and *Inside Network Marketing*.
- is a sales trainer and speaker.
- has a B.A. in Speech and Theatre from the University of Michigan and a J.D. from Southwestern University School of Law.
- worked at Universal Studios and United Artists.
- has written for movies and TV.
- lives with his wife, Marlyn, and their son, Seth, in California.

www.artburleigh.com
1-818-725-4210

How to Contact
Art Burleigh and Jan Ruhe

*True Leadership—How you can provide it
and become secure, happy and rich!*

Order this powerful book through our web sites or by calling or writing either of us.

Attractive volume discounts are available.

Our web sites also offer information about our worldwide *True Leadership* Training Seminars and other fabulous tools and resources to accelerate your business success and personal growth.

Art Burleigh	**Jan Ruhe**
21704 Devonshire Street	300 Puppy Smith
PMB 287	Suite 203-290
Chatsworth, CA 91311	Aspen, CO 81611
U.S.A.	U.S.A.
Phone: 818-725-4210	Phone: 970-927-3010
Fax: 818-709-6252	Fax: 970-927-0200
www.artburleigh.com	**www.janruhe.com**